Love

One

Another

Fulton J. Sheen

Bishop Sheen Today
280 John Street
Midland, Ontario, Canada, L4R 2J5
www.bishopsheentoday.com

Sheen, Fulton J. (Fulton John), 1895-1979. Love One Another. Registered in the name of P.J. Kenedy & Sons under Library of Congress catalog card number: A 184314, following publication October 31, 1944.

Title: Love One Another, Fulton J. Sheen,
author; edited by Allan J. Smith.

Description: Midland, Ontario: Bishop Sheen
Today, 2023.

Includes bibliographical references.

Identifiers:
ISBN: 978-1-990427-99-2 (paperback)
ISBN: 978-1-998229-03-1 (hardcover)
ISBN: 978-1-998229-01-7 (e-book)

Subjects: God – Love – Christian - Jews –
Protestants -

"I have called you friends …
A new commandment I give
unto you: That you love one
another, As I have loved you".

(John 15:15; 13:34)

DEDICATED TO MARY

GRACIOUS MOTHER

OF THE DIVINE CHRIST

WHO PROMISED NOT TO MAKE

US SERVANTS BUT FRIENDS

CONTENTS

INTRODUCTION

Archbishop Fulton J. Sheen was a man for all seasons. Over his lifetime, he spent himself for souls, transforming lives with the clear teaching of the truths of Christ and His Church through his books, radio addresses, lectures, television series, and his many newspaper columns.

As a much sought-after lecturer, his topics ranged from the social concerns of the day to matters of faith and morals. With an easy and personable manner, Sheen could strike up a conversation on just about any subject, making numerous friends as well as converts.

During his presentations, Archbishop Sheen would offer his trademark words of benediction, "God love you". Sheen explained that this phrase "God love you" means God is love, God loves you, and you ought to love God in return.

Along with his familiar parting phrase of "God love you", Archbishop Sheen was known for beginning his lectures with the greeting "Friends". This salutation had a twofold meaning: he was referring to the scripture passage "I no longer call you servants ... instead, I have called you friends." (John 15:15). And, he wanted to make friends with men and women of all faiths, in the hope of gradually helping them to come to know the Lord Jesus Christ.

With love as its central focus, this anthology begins with a collection of essays and prayers compiled by Fulton Sheen under the title *'Love One Another'*. (Published by P.J. Kenedy & Sons, New York in 1944.)

In these writings, Sheen speaks to Catholics, Protestants, and Jews regarding the fostering of friendships between various religious groups.

Additionally, he makes several practical suggestions on how to improve relations between people of varying backgrounds. An array of reflections is presented for devotional inspiration, simultaneously laying out a groundwork in spiritual values proven to facilitate harmonious relationships.

The are some who have considered this work a 'must-read' for those sincerely interested in seeking the attainment of a genuine brotherhood of man. Others may find in this collection, some prayerful and practical solutions to many of today's most challenging interpersonal problems.

Archbishop Fulton Sheen made it clear that the command given by Jesus 'to love your neighbor as yourself', is clearly an effective answer to combating the sin of intolerance.

During one of his radio addresses in 1944, Archbishop Sheen fondly said, "I have always addressed you as friends, and you know that unseen friends are sometimes the best friends. To say 'my friends', would be to claim a privilege. But friends are the expression of a hope. A hope that by listening to me, I may with traitorous trueness and with loyal deceit, betray you into the hands of the God of Love and Mercy."

Friends, "A new commandment I give to you, that you love one another; even as I have loved you, and that you also love one another. By this, all men will know that you are my disciples if you have love for one another." (John 13:34-35)

THE FOUNDATION OF LOVE — GOD

"Man came from the beast; therefore he ought to love his fellowman."

How silly that sounds! Everyone knows that the law of the survival of the fittest can never evolve into love, nor can the struggle for existence develop into human brotherhood. If we come from the beasts, then we may appropriately be expected to act like beasts.

Start with another philosophy of life, that love originates in heaven. "A new commandment I give unto you, that you love one another; that as I have loved you, you also love one another. By this will all men know that you are my disciples, if you have love for one another." (John 13: 34-35)

Loving one another is now reasonable, because the God of love made us, because the God of love redeemed us, and because the God of love sanctified us.

What does it mean to say that God is love?

Love is, a) mutual self-giving, b) which ends in self-realization. Love first of all involves reciprocity and "otherness." A love that cannot diffuse itself is not love for love raised to its highest power is a mutual self-giving.

All love, therefore, implies generation: the giving not of what one has, but of what one is.

Perfect love is an Act. Sterile, selfish love is the negation of love. A love that refuses to propagate itself is not love. Goodness is necessarily social.

Secondly, perfect love is not merely mutual self-giving; otherwise, it might end in exhaustion. There must, therefore, be added to the idea of giving that of self-recovery.

In addition to the Source that gives and the Stream that flows from it, there must be the Sea in which all is recovered without loss, and without cessation.

Raised to the infinite, the Love that generates is the Father; the Love that is generated from all eternity is the Son. That such Love would there end would be less than loving. Love must circle back upon itself, and that eternal bond of love uniting Father and Son is called the Holy Spirit.

To put it in other words, I can know something of the existence of God, something of His Infinite Power, Life, and Beauty by contemplating His universe, but I could never divine anything of His secret Thought and Love unless He told me. His creation gives but dim hints of these.

It was, therefore, only natural that man should desire further knowledge of the inner life of God and, in seeking that light, would ask such questions as Plato asked four centuries before Christ:

"If there is only one God, what does He think about? If He is an intelligent being, He must think of something.

"If there is only one God, whom does He love, for to be happy one must love?"

These questions were hurled against the high heavens as so much brass, for there was no man to give them an answer. The answer could come only from God Himself, and it came when Our Blessed Lord appeared on earth and revealed to us the inmost life of God, namely, there are three Persons in God, God the Father, God the Son, and God the Holy Ghost. This tremendous mystery is known as the Trinity.

If we would answer the questions of Plato and know what God thinks about, and whom God loves, let us first ask the questions of man, for man has been made to the image and likeness of God. The study of man's thought and man's will should tell us something about the thought and the will of God.

Of the thought of man, three things may be said, viz.: It is a word; it is generated or born; and it is personal.

Man thinks; he thinks a thought, such as "Justice," "Faith," "Fortitude," or "Charity." Now, these thoughts are words; they are words even before I speak them, for the vocal word is only the expression of the internal word in my mind.

These thoughts or internal words are generated or born. Who, for example, ever sat down to a meal with "Justice"? Who ever heard of "Charity" going out for a walk? Who knows the size, the weight, and the color of "Fortitude"?

No one has ever seen, tasted, or touched these thoughts, and yet they are real. They are spiritual thoughts.

But where did they come from? Since they are not wholly in the outside world, they must have been produced, or generated, by the mind itself; not with that physical birth by which animal produces animal, but by a spiritual generation by which we produce ideas or internal words.

There are other ways of begetting life, we must remember, than physically. The most chaste way that life is begotten is the way in which thoughts and ideas are born in the mind.

Finally, the thoughts of man are personal. Some thoughts of man are banal and commonplace, trite thoughts which no man remembers; but there are also thoughts which are spirit and life.

There are some thoughts of man into which man puts his very soul and his very being, all that he has been and all that he is, which thoughts are so much his own individual thoughts as to carry his personality and his spirit with them and to be recognizable as such.

Thus we say, "that is a thought of Pascal, of Bossuet, of Shakespeare, or of Dante."

Now apply these three reflections about human thought to God. God thinks a thought, and that thought is a Word; it is generated or born and is therefore called a Son, and finally, that Word or Son is Personal.

God thinks; He thinks a Thought. This thought of God is a Word, as my own thought is called a word after it is pronounced. It is an internal word. But

God's thought is not like ours. It is not multiple.

God does not think one thought, or one word, one minute and another the next. Thoughts are not born to die, and do not die to be reborn in the mind of God. All is present to Him at once. In Him, there is only one word. He has no need of another.

That thought or word is infinite and equal to Himself, unique and absolute, first-born of the Spirit of God; a word from which all human words have been derived, and of which created things are merely the broken syllables or letters; a Word which is the source of all the Wisdom in the world.

The latest scientific discoveries, the new knowledge of the great expanse of the heavens, the sciences of biology, physics, and chemistry, the more lofty sciences of meta-physics, philosophy and theology — the knowledge of the Shepherds, and the knowledge of the Wise Men — all this knowledge has its source in the word or the wisdom of God.

The Infinite Thought of God is called not only a Word to indicate that it is the Wisdom of God, but it is also called a Son because it has been generated or begotten.

The thought or the word of God does not come from the outside world; it is born in His Spirit in a much more perfect way than the thought of "Justice" is generated by my spirit.

The giving of life or the power of birth, I repeat, is not limited to human beings. In the language of Sacred Scripture, "Shall not I, that make others to bring forth children, Myself bring forth?" saith the Lord. "Shall I Who give generation to others myself be barren?"

The ultimate Source of all generation or birth is God, Whose Word is born of Him and therefore is called a Son.

Just as in our own human order, the principle of all generation is called the Father, so, too, in the Trinity the principle of all generation is called the Father, and the one generated is called the Son because

He is the perfect Image and Resemblance of the Father.

If an earthly father can transmit to his son all the nobility of his character, and all the fine traits of his life, how much more so can the Heavenly Father communicate to His own Eternal Son all the nobility, the perfection, and the eternity of His Being!

Finally, this Word or Son, begotten of the Eternal God, is personal. The thought of God is not commonplace, but reaches to the abyss of all that is known or can be known. Into this Thought of Word God puts Himself so entirely that it is as living as Himself.

If a human genius can put his whole personality into a thought, in a more perfect way God is able to put so much of Himself into a thought that that Thought or Word or Son is conscious of Himself and is a Divine Person.

The Father does not first exist and then think; the Father and Son are co-eternal for in God all is present and unchanging.

Nothing is new and nothing is lost. Thus it is that the Father, contemplating His Image, His Word, His Son, can say in the ecstasy of the first and real paternity: "Thou art My Son; this day have I begotten Thee."

"This day" — this day of eternity, that is, the indivisible duration of being without end. "This day," in that act that will never end, as it has never begun; "this day" — the agelessness of eternity.

Go back to the origin of the world, pile century on century, aeon on aeon, age on age: "The Word was with God." Go back before the creation of the angels, before Michael summoned his war hosts *to* victory with a flash of archangelic spears; even then, "The Word was with God."

It is that Word which St. John heard in the beginning of his Gospel, when he wrote: "In the beginning was the Word: and the Word was with God; and the Word was God."

Just as my interior thoughts are not made manifest without a word, so the

Word in the language of John, "became flesh and dwelt amongst us."

And the Word is no other than the Second Person of the Blessed Trinity, the Word Who embraces the beginning and end of all things; the Word Who existed before creation; the Word Who presided at creation as the King of the Universe, the Word made flesh at Bethlehem, the Word made flesh on the Cross, and the Word made flesh dwelling in His divinity and humanity in the Eucharistic Emmanuel.

The Good Friday of twenty centuries ago did not mark the end of Him, as it did not mark the beginning. It is one of the moments of the Eternal Word of God.

Jesus Christ has a pre-history — a pre-history not to be studied in the rocks of the earth, nor in the caves of man, nor in the slime and dust of primeval jungles, but in the bosom of an Eternal Father.

He alone brought pre-history to history; He alone has dated all the records of human events into two periods: the period before, and the period after His coming.

If we would ever deny that the Word became Flesh, and that the Son of God became the Son of man, we would have to date our denial as over one thousand nine hundred years after His coming.

We are not yet finished with the inner life of God, for if God is the source of all life and truth and goodness in the world, He must have a will as well as an intellect; a love as well as a thought. It is a fact of nature that every being loves its own perfection.

The perfection of the eye is color, and it loves the beauty of the sun setting in the flaming monstrance of the west; the perfection of the ear is sound, and it loves the harmony of an overture of Beethoven or a sonata of Chopin.

Love has two terms: He Who loves and He Who is loved. In love the two are reciprocal. I love and I am loved. Between me and the one, I love there is a bond.

It is not my love; it is not his love; it is our love; the mysterious resultant of two affections, a bond which enchains, and an embrace wherein two hearts leap with but a single Joy.

The Father loves the Son, the Image of His Perfection and the Son loves the Father. Love is not only in the Father. Love is not only in the Son. There is something between them, as it were.

The Father loves the Son, Whom He engenders. The Son loves the Father, Who engendered Him. They contemplate each other; love each other in a love so powerful, so strong, and so perfect that it forms between them a living bond.

They give themselves in a love so infinite that, like the truth which expresses itself only in the giving of a whole personality, their love can express itself in nothing less than a Person, who is Love.

Love at such a stage does not speak; does not cry; does not express itself by words, nor by canticles; it expresses itself as we do in some ineffable moments, by that which indicates the very exhaustion of our giving: namely, a sigh, or a breath — and that is why the Third Person of the Blessed

Trinity is called the Holy Spirit of the Holy Ghost.

That breath of love is not a passing one as our own, but an Eternal Spirit. How all this is done, I know not, but on the testimony of God revealing, I know that this same Holy Spirit overshadowed the Blessed Virgin Mary, and He Who was born of her was called the Son of God.

It was the same Spirit of Whom our Lord spoke to Nicodemus when He told him he must be born again of "water and the Holy Ghost."

It was the same Spirit Whom Our Blessed Saviour gave to His Apostles with the words, "Receive ye the Holy Ghost: whose sins you shall forgive, they are forgiven them."

It was the same Spirit of Whom Our Lord spoke at the Last Supper: "He shall glorify me, because He shall receive of mine, and shall show it to you. All things whatsoever the Father hath, are Mine."

In this passage, Christ tells His disciples that the Holy Spirit, Who is to come, will in the future reveal divine knowledge which has been communicated to Him in His Pocession from both the Father and Son.

It is that same Spirit Who, in fulfillment of the promise, "when the Spirit of Truth is come, He will teach you all truth," descended on the Apostles on the day of Pentecost, and became the soul of the Church.

The continuous, unbroken succession of the truth communicated by Christ to His Church has survived to our own day, not because of the human organization of the Church, for that is carried on by frail vessels, but because of the profusion of the Spirit of Love and Truth over Christ's Vicar, and all who belong to Christ's mystical Body, which is His Church.

Three in one, Father, Son, and Holy Ghost; three persons in one God; one essence, distinction of persons — such is the mystery of the Trinity; such is the inner life of God.

Just as I am, I know, and I love, and yet I am one; as the three angles of a triangle do not make three triangles but one; as the heat, power, and light of the sun do not make three suns, but one; as water, ice and steam are all manifestations of the one substance; as the form, color and perfume of the rose do not make three roses, but one; as our soul, our intellect and our will do not make three substances, but one; as one times one times one times one does not equal three, but one — so, too, in some much more mysterious way, there are three Persons in God, and yet only one God.

The Trinity is the answer to the questions of Plato. If there is only one God, what does He think about? He thinks an eternal thought, or about His Eternal Son. If there is only one God, whom does He love? He loves His Son, and that mutual love is the Holy Spirit.

The great philosopher was fumbling about for the mystery of the Trinity. His great mind seemed in some small way to suspect that an infinite being must have relations of thought and love, and that God cannot be conceived without thought and love.

But it was not until the Word became Incarnate, that man knew the secret of those relations and the inner life of God.

It is that mystery of the Trinity which gives the answer to those who have pictured God as an egotist God, sitting in solitary splendor before the world began, for the Trinity is a revelation that before creation God enjoyed the amiable society of His three Persons, the infinite communion with Truth and the embrace of infinite Love, and hence had no need ever to go outside Himself in search for happiness.

The greatest wonder of all is that, being perfect and enjoying perfect happiness, He ever should have made a world. If He did make a world, He could only have had one motive for making it. It could not add to His perfection; it could not add to His truth; it could not increase His happiness. He made a world only *because He loved.*

Finally, it is the mystery of the Trinity which gives the answer to our quest for happiness and the true meaning of Heaven.

Heaven is not a place where there is the mere vocal repetition of alleluias or the monotonous fingering of harps. Heaven is a place where we find the fullness of the joys of earth.

Heaven is a place where we find in its plenitude those things which slake the thirst of hearts, satisfy the hunger of starving minds, and give rest to unrequited love.

Heaven is the communion with perfect Life, perfect Truth, and perfect Love, God the Father, God the Son, and God the Holy Ghost to whom be all honor and glory forever and ever. Amen.

God chose not to keep the secret of His Power to Himself, but told it to nothingness — and this was Creation. God chose not to keep the Beauty of His Intellect and Will, but to communicate a likeness of it to creatures — and these are angels and men.

Love wills not to keep the secrets of His Wisdom to Himself but tells them to man — and this is Revelation.

Love tends to become like the one loved, and since God loved man, God became man — and this is the Person of Jesus Christ, true God, and true man.

Love seeks to take another's pain and sin as its own and thus to make it whole — and this was the Cross and Redemption.

Love seeks not only to give what it has, but even to communicate its very Spirit — and this was Pentecost and the Birthday of the Church.

SOME CHARACTERISTICS
OF GOD'S LOVE

The Love of God is Justice!

How could God be good if He loved the bad equally with the good? The essence of love is not indifference to morality. "The way of the wicked is an abomination to the Lord: he that followeth justice is beloved by him." (Prov. 15:9)

"You have wearied the Lord with your words, and you said: Wherein have we wearied him? In that you say: 'Every one that doth evil, is good in the sight of the Lord, and such please him': or 'surely where is the God of judgment?'" (Mal. 2:17)

The Love of God is Freedom!

How could love be love if it were forced? By making man free, God made it possible for man to reject Divine Love. Man cannot be made to love God any more that he can be made to enjoy Bach's classical music. The power of choice is not necessarily the choice of what is best. Hence, "If you love me, keep my commandments." (John 14:15)

The Love of God is the First Cause of all Things!

Though God is the First Cause of all things, man is a secondary and instrumental cause, and not a mere robot. God wrote a wonderful drama and gave it to free men to play, and sometimes they make a botch of it. Not in time, but at the end of the world, all things will be restored according to Justice. "For because sentence is not speedily pronounced against the evil, the children of men commit evils without any fear. But though a sinner do evil a hundred times, and by patience be borne withal, I know from thence that it shall be well with them that fear God, who dread his face." (Ecc. 8:11-12)

The Love of God is Eternal!

Therefore, I can never escape it. I can tend toward it freely and thus receive mercy, or I can freely rebel against it and in my frustration feel His Justice. "For we must all be manifested before the judgment seat of Christ, that every one may receive the proper things of the body, according as he hath done, whether it be good or evil." (2 Cor. 5:10)

The Love of God is All-Powerful!

God would never have given men the power to choose evil if He could not draw goodness out of evil. The power to crucify Christ is *mine,* but the effect of that crucifixion, namely, the conquest of death by resurrection, is not mine, but God's. "There is no wisdom, there is no prudence, there is no counsel against the Lord. The horse is prepared for the day of battle: but the Lord giveth safety." (Prov. 21:30-31)

The Love of God is All-Seeing!

"Every man that passeth beyond his own bed, despising his own soul, and saying: Who seeth me? Darkness compasseth me about, and the walls cover me, and no man seeth me; whom do I fear? The most High will not remember my sins. And he understandeth not that His eye seeth all things for such a man's fear driveth from him the fear of God, and the eyes of man fearing him: And he knoweth not that the eyes of the Lord are far brighter ... For all things were known to the Lord God before they were created: so also after they were perfected he beholdeth all things." (Sirach 23:25, 29)

The Love of God is Strong!

Love is not "broadmindedness." Capacity for indignation is sometimes a test of love, for there are enormities which true love must not only challenge, but resist. The sun which warms so gently can also wither; the rain which nourishes so tenderly can also rot. The change is not in the sun or the rain: it is in that upon which it falls. So the Love of God to the good is love; to the wicked, it seems wrath. "For we know that the judgment of God is, according to truth, against them that do such things ... Or despisest thou the riches of his goodness, and patience and long- suffering? Knowest thou not that the benignity of God leadeth thee to penance? But according to thy hardness and impenitent heart, thou treasurest up to thyself wrath, against the day of wrath,

30

and revelation of the just judgment of God." (Rom. 2:2, 4, 5)

The Love of God is Merciful!

If we had never sinned, we never could have called Christ "Saviour." "But thou hast mercy upon all, because thou canst do all things, and overlookest the sins of men for the sake of repentance. For thou lovest all things that are, and hatest none of the things which thou hast made: for thou didst not appoint, or make anything hating it." (Wis. 11:24, 25)

The Love of God is the Cause of Our Love!

There are sparks of love in us because there was first the Flame in God. "Jesus answered, and said to her: Whosoever drinketh of this water, shall thirst again; but he that shall drink of the water that I will give him, shall not thirst for ever: But the water that I will give him, shall become in him a fountain of water, springing up into life everlasting." (John 4:13, 14)

SOME CHARACTERISTICS OF GOD'S LOVE

The Love of God Rules the Universe

Because all things in the world, from atoms to angels, were made by Love, it follows that the whole universe seeks and moves toward its own perfection and its own good. Acorns tend to become good oaks; two atoms of hydrogen and one atom of oxygen united by an electrical spark tend to become water.

Inasmuch as all things have a natural inclination the perfection befitting their nature, they tend in some way to become like God. Scientists only *discover* the laws of nature; they do not *invent* them.

The chemical and biological laws which govern animals are all participations in the Eternal Reason and Love of God. They act for a purpose, that is, according to reason because Eternal Reason created them; they seek their own good because Eternal Goodness or Divine Love called them into being.

The Love of God Made a Moral Universe!

But Divine Love acted differently when He created Man. Water *must* seek its own level, but man *ought* to be good. A stone cannot choose to fly upwards when released from my hand, but a man can choose to disobey the law of his nature. In other words, lower nature is determined, and therefore amoral; man is free, and therefore moral.

God *compels* the stone to obey the law of gravitation, but He does not *compel* us to be good. How could we really love if we were forced?

Is it not the possibility of a "No" that gives so much charm to our "Yes"? God, therefore, gave us the power to seek deliberately a goal and purpose other than His Perfect Love, in order that there might be meaning in our allegiance and love when we freely choose to give it. To man alone on this earth did God communicate some of His Freedom.

And if it be asked: "If God knew that I would rebel against His love and be a sinner, why did He make me?" The answer is: God did not make you as a sinner. You made yourself a sinner. In that sense, you are your own creator.

The possibility, not the necessity, of moral evil, of wars and social injustices which follow them, is the price we have to pay for the greatest good we possess — the gift of freedom. God could, of course, at any moment stop a war, but only at a terrible cost — the destruction of human freedom.

There are only two things that could possibly remove evil and suffering from the world: either the conformity of human wills to the will of God, or God becoming a dictator and destroying all human wills.

Why is it that men, who by forgetting the Love of God turn the universe into a house of mass-suicide, never think of blaming themselves, but immediately put God on the judgment seat, and question His Love and Goodness?

We all have a share in the evils of the world, and it ill behooves us to ignore our faults and become critics of God. It is we who are in the prisoners' dock in a world crisis like this. Instead of questioning the God of Love, we ought to be throwing ourselves on the Mercy of His Judgment.

MAN FLEEING GOD'S LOVE

These are several ways to avoid loving God.

Deny that you are a sinner.

Say that "no one believes in sin today," or "the sense of guilt is oppressive." If you are a fallen-away Catholic say: "I no longer believe in Confession."

Introduce speculative or theoretical questions to escape the implications of your moral bankruptcy and the primal, basic, inescapable fact that you have sinned against the love of God.

Thus you will avoid entertaining in your conscience the necessity of confession.

This is what the woman at the well did when Our Lord, with a touch of moral realism, reminded her that she had five husbands. She evaded the issue of personal sin by raising the question of whether one ought to worship at Gerizim or Jerusalem.

Be like her. Make religion a controversy rather than a conversion. What you want is an argument but what you need is absolution. By confusing the two, you can avoid meeting the God of love until the day of your death.

Pretend that religion is for the ignorant and the superstitious, but not for the truly learned such as yourself.

Hearing Our Lord preaching in the Temple, some asked: "How doth this man know letters, having never learned?" (John 7:15) Here was the same snobbishness as in an earlier question: "Can anything of good come from Nazareth?" (John 1:46)

Be concerned as they were, with the social background of those who teach religion, or with its intellectual tone rather than its *moral emphasis* and *spiritual intention.* Say that "one religion is just as good as another," which is a clever way of implying that one is just as bad as another.

Boast of your "broadmindedness" and condemn the "intolerance" of everyone who has definite convictions. Dwell on no planet, but survey them all.

When religion must be discussed, always begin with, "Now this is *my* idea of religion," thus avoiding the problem of what is *God's* idea of religion. You thus reflect yourself in your own opinion.

Judge religions by whether they are "progressive" or "reactionary", "modern" or "medieval"; but never on the basis on whether they are "true" or "false." Boast of *where* you got your A.B., rather than *what* you learned. Make it appear that your superior knowledge of comparative religions makes the comparison of religions useless.

Conceal the fact that in reality, you belong to the *intelligentsia* — *those* who have been educated beyond their intelligence.

Smile when you hear the text of Our Lord, "I praise Thee, Father, Lord of heaven and earth, that thou hast hidden these things from the wise and prudent, and hast revealed them to little *ones.*" (Luke 10:21) And above all else when you wish to avoid discussing the spiritual life of the Catholic Church, libel it by saying it is "Fascist"!

Insist that the sole purpose of religion is social service.

When Our Lord fed the multitude, many crossed the lake to make Him King, but He answered: "Amen, amen, I say to you, you seek me, not because you have seen miracles, but because you did eat of the loaves and were filled. Labour not for meat which perisheth, but for that which endureth unto life everlasting, which the Son of Man will give you. For him hath God the Father sealed." (John 6:26-27)

But when He talked to them about Bread from Heaven, they said His religion was absurd. Life, they insisted, consists in being well fed. Think of religion solely as an "ambulance" to care for the economically unfed, until science and progress can dispense with it.

When the Church proposes a social solution based on spiritual regeneration, say "the Church is political." When it abstains from a political policy, say "the Church is too unworldly." Quote Marx: "religion is the opium of the people."

Make it appear that Christianity is a means to social justice, rather than its cause. Above all else, condemn the Church for its attitude on artificial Birth Control. "After all, if God gave us bodies, He intended we should use them."

Then you escape that moral problem of the soul and render inapplicable the words of Our Lord: "For what doth it profit a man, if he gain the whole world, and suffer the loss of his own soul?" (Matt. 16:26) Of course, you will miss all the consolations of religion for the Master said: "And fear ye not them that kill the body and are not able to kill the soul. But rather fear him that can destroy both soul and body in hell." (Matt. 10:28)

Judge religion by whether or not it is accepted by the "important" people of the world.

When the masses crowded around Our Lord, the Pharisees sent ministers to apprehend Him. When the ministers returned empty-handed the Pharisees asked them: "Are you also seduced? Hath any one of the rulers believed in him, or of the Pharisees?" (John 7:47-48) They judged religion by the *elite* rather than by the *elect*.

Once therefore you become convinced of the truth of the Church, do not join it, lest you lose your job, or lest you be ridiculed by the world.

Some of the chiefs of the people believed in Our Lord, "but ... they did not confess Him ... for they loved the glory of men rather than the glory of God." (John 12:42-43)

If an important man does embrace the Church, explain it away as "momentary insanity"; when a young woman enters the convent to dedicate her life to God, say: "She must have been disappointed in love."

By so doing, you will always avoid discussing the eternal.

Concentrate on the idea that a Church which is not well-received by the world cannot be true, thus avoiding the retort of the Saviour: "I have chosen you out of the world, therefore the world hateth you." (John 15:19)

Avoid all contemplation, self-examination, and inquiry into the moral state of your soul.

Never be alone with yourself lest your conscience carry on an unbearable repartee. Cultivate a love of crowds, excitement, and noise. Thus will you be defended against "despairing scruples" and "silly qualms" and "remorse."

Shout down the whispers of Heaven. Alcohol may help extinguish the sparks of a few actual graces of God suggesting that you are not on the right track.

Make your business your religion, and then you will not have to make religion your business.

At night when you lie awake and are utterly alone with your soul, never give it a thought. Maybe you can escape the consequences of your life by not thinking about it.

If the thoughts of God get too strong, console yourself with the idea that "good" and "evil" are subjective and psychological. A good joke about hell is always a good way to avoid dwelling on its possibility.

Call yourself a "heretic"; ridicule the pure as "Puritanical"; the clean of mouth as "devoid of a sense of humor"; but the best way of all to avoid serious thinking about religion is to say: "I've been through all that," as if there is nothing more to be said.

From that point on, the invitation of the Saviour seems stupid: "Come to me, all you that labour and are burdened, and I will refresh you, Take up my yoke upon you, and learn of me, because I am meek and humble of heart; and you shall find rest to your souls. For my yoke is sweet, and my burden light." (Matt. 11:28-30)

Take yourself very seriously.

Be proud of what you *have* rather than what you *are;* of what you *know* rather than what you *do;* of what you *did* rather than what you *ought to have done.*

If you cannot convince others that you know everything, then at least convince them that they know nothing. If you cannot lay claim to *omniscience,* you can probably make them admit their *nescience.*

There is no better way to keep God out of your soul than to be full of self. If you know all, how can God teach you anything? You escape the problem of faith by boasting of the capacities of your reason.

Say that you are too intelligent to believe in sin, and thus you avoid discussing redemption, for if you never

45

did wrong, it is utterly stupid to suggest that someone could make you right.

Be a connoisseur of all churches in virtue of your superior wisdom, and you thus escape the obligation of joining any. Art critics do not paint. Why should religious critics be religious?

Keep your conceit always at a high level, for thus will you never be forced to admit that you are conceited. By the same token, you will succeed in identifying religion with infantilism.

You can even quote in your own support the words of Our Lord: "Amen I say to you, unless you turn and become as little children, you shall not enter into the kingdom of heaven. Whosoever, therefore, shall humble himself as this little child, he is the greater in the kingdom of heaven." (Matt. 18:3-4)

GOD'S LOVE PURSUING MAN

Though we may not always be on the quest of God, God is always on the quest of us. Even experiences and moments not of themselves calculated to spiritualize us, God in His Mercy may use to throw us back to Him. Thus:

Satiety

God calls the soul to Himself in the feeling of disgust. The very feeling following sin, the emptiness which sin engenders, God may use to summon us to be filled with His grace.

An animal seeks pleasure within the finite limits of his physical organism; but man wants it to satisfy the infinite thirst of his soul. In man, therefore, the law of diminishing returns operates: As pleasure decreases, the desire for it increases. Pleasures then begin to exasperate because they "lie"; they do not give what they promised. Sadness, bitterness, and cynicism sometimes seize the soul, and with it a fatigue of life. That very emptiness can be the foundation of conversion. The desire for happiness could not be wrong. It must be, therefore, that we sought happiness in the wrong objects: in creatures apart from God, instead of in creatures under God's law. Thus, in the very confusion and disgust following sin is hidden a sense of awakened spiritual possibilities. A soul is on the verge of knowing itself when it knows that acting like a beast it *might* live like an angel. After having fed himself on husks, the prodigal began to yearn for the bread of the father's house.

Sacrifice

The self-indulgent soul which surrounds itself with every comfort and luxury, while making other persons means to its convenience, sometimes has its depths shattered by the sight of someone else living happily and peacefully amidst surroundings of complete self-forgetfulness and service for others. "I could be like that," or "I wish I were as happy as that person." The crust of egotism is broken and there gushes forth the awful beauty of self-surrender. The soul for the first time comes to realize the sublime truth of Our Lord's words, that the best way to save life is to lose it. Such a consciousness is an actual grace of God, and if acted upon throws great light on the darkened cover of our soul.

Suffering

Many persons identify themselves with their environment. Because life is good to them, they believe they are good. They never dwell on eternity because time is so pleasant. When suffering strikes, they become divorced from their pleasant surroundings and are left naked in their own souls. They then see that they were not really affable and genial, but irritable and impatient. When the sun of outer prosperity sank, they had no inner light to guide their darkened souls. It is, therefore, not what happens to us that matters; it is how we react to it.

No one is better because of pain; conceivably a man may become seared and scarred by pain. But, the very emptiness of soul that follows enforced divorce from pleasurable surroundings does drive the soul back unto itself, and if it cooperates with grace at that moment, it may find the meaning of life. It was through a wound that Saint Ignatius came to know himself. Many in life do not meet Christ until, like the thief on the right, they find Him on a Cross. On the battlefields in war many a man has found Him the only One to whom to turn.

Age

The young are full of hopes for life is full of promise. The sophomore thinks that science can take the place of God, that progress is necessary and not conditioned on discipline, and that pleasure is the goal of living. Later on, when one has left the hills of religion behind, and gone down into the plains where secular hopes were to be fulfilled, one becomes disillusioned by the monotony and routine of life. A moment comes when the soul begins to look back to those hills of religion, as to a happiness left behind. The fleeting years now seem to the soul as a thief in the house, explaining many losses which were never before. The soul is awakened; great possibilities lie ahead — for: "Not till the fire is dying in the grate, look we for any kinship with the stars."

Impact with a Sinful World

All the modern explanations given for the existence of evil fail to fit the facts. Biologists told us evil was due to a fall in evolution, but if progress is inevitable why have there been two World Wars in twenty-one years?

Sociologists told us evil was due to systems: Capitalism or Communism or Nazism or Fascism. How could the world adopt evil systems if minds were not already fit soil for their growth? Since evil is so universal, must it not be due to a breakdown of a universal moral law? Is not the world in a mess for the same reason I am in a mess, namely, because I have not done what I *ought* to have done?

Is not this precisely what Christianity means, that God had to come down from Heaven to earth to make it right.

Christianity does not begin in comfort but in catastrophe. Once a soul begins to realize that the world is rotten because it has broken the moral law of God, it has taken the first step toward conversion. God and the soul can meet on the roadway of a broken and disordered World. Such is the meaning of Bethlehem and Calvary.

Contact with the Divine Presence

Sometimes it has happened that a man who had never given a thought to religion entered a Catholic Church and although he knew nothing of her teaching, after half an hour or more spent in the presence of the Blessed Sacrament, was seized with a sense that "Something or Someone is there" that makes the church different. Such a soul does not know or believe that Our Lord is really and truly present on the altar of every Catholic Church. He does know that he feels "impelled" to remain in that mysterious Presence. Like the disciples of Emmaus, the soul has been companioning with the Saviour without knowing it. The investigation of the reasons behind the sense of the sacred in this and similar experiences may lead to the fulness of faith.

Sadness

Why do we love to see, on the stage or screen, doleful and tragical things which we never would want to befall us? Why should sorrow be our pleasure and tears be our satisfaction? Why do we weep for the fanciful on the stage, but not for the reality? Why do we, who would have none of our friends murdered, love to read about murders? Do men who are at peace want to see feigned misery'? Do those who are glad rejoice in pretended tragedy?

Is not our desire to see that which is sad or tragic a revelation of the sadness and tragedy of our own souls? A soul that loves God and sees misery wants to relieve it; a soul that has abandoned God and sees misery wants to weep over it, not knowing that he is really weeping over himself. We act as mourners when we really are the mourned.

The moment we realize that our sadness is born of our sins, we are ripe for conversion. Then we feel the poignancy of the invitation: "Come to me, all you that labour, and are burdened, and I will refresh you." (Matt. 11:28)

O WHITHER SHALL I FLY

O Whither shall I fly? what path untrod
Shall I seek out to 'scape the flaming rod
Of my offended, of my angry God?

'Tis vain to *flee;* 'tis neither here nor there
Can 'scape that hand, until that hand forbear;
Ah me! where is he not, that's ev'rywhere?

'Tis vain to flee, till gentle mercy show
Her better eye; the farther off we go,
The swing of Justice deals the mightier blow.

The ingenuous child, corrected, doth not fly
His angry mother's hand, but clings more high,
And quenches with his tears her flaming eye.

Great God! there is no safety here below;
Thou art my fortress, thou that seem'st my foe.

'Tis thou, that strik'st the stroke, must guard
the blow.

Thou art my God, by thee I fall or stand;
Thy grace hath given me courage to withstand
All tortures, but my conscience and thy hand.

I know thy justice is thyself; I know,
Just God, thy very self is mercy too;
If not to thee, where, whither shall I go?

Francis Quarles

THE PULLEY

When God at first made man,
Having a glass of blessings standing by,
"Let us," said He, "pour on him all we can;
Let the world's riches, which dispersed lie,
Contract Into a span."

So strength first made a way;
Then beauty flow'd, then wisdom, honour,
pleasure;
When almost all was out, God made a stay,
Perceiving that, alone of all His treasure, Rest
in the bottom lay.

"For if I should," said He,
"Bestow this jewel also on My creature,

He would adore My gifts instead of me,
And rest in Nature, not the God of Nature:
So both should losers be.

"Yet let him keep the rest,
But keep them with repining restlessness;
Let him be rich and weary, that at least,
If goodness lead him not, yet weariness
May toss him to My breast."

George Herbert

"IF I COULD SHUT THE GATE"

If I could shut the gate against my thoughts
And keep out sorrow from this room, within,
Or memory could cancel all the notes
Of my misdeeds, and I unthink my sin:
How free, how clear, how clean my soul should
lie,
Discharged of such a loathsome company!

Or were there other rooms without my heart
That did not to my conscience join so near,
Where I might lodge the thoughts of sin apart
That I might not their clamorous crying hear,
What peace, what joy, what ease should I
possess,
Freed from their horrors that my soul oppress!

But, O my Saviour, Who my refuge art,
Let Thy dear mercies stand 'twixt them and me,
And be the wall to separate my heart
So that I may at length repose me free;
That peace, and joy, and rest may be within,
And I remain divided from my sin.

Anonymous

DIVINE FRIENDSHIP

Though man is human, he may live on a threefold level: subhuman, human, and divine.

The Subhuman Level

We never say to a monkey when he acts foolish: "Do not act like a nut," because the monkey has not the power to lower himself to a sub-monkey level. But to a man, we can say: "Do not act like a monkey" because a man sometimes can fail to be all that he *ought* to be; he can lower himself to a subhuman level. A fall from a higher state is not possible to the beast, but it is possible for man; a monkey can never be a nut, but a man can be a beast.

Man lives on this subhuman level in several ways: When he denies he has a soul and thus identifies himself with the animal; when he affirms that he has no other destiny than to disintegrate with the dust; and when he bases his life on the principle that the sole purpose of living is the satisfaction of his animal impulses.

The Human Level

A man begins to live a human existence when he recognizes a *specific* difference between himself and animals, namely, possession of an intellect which can understand Truth and a will which can choose Goodness. As a human being, he bends subhuman things to his will; for example, he makes his body the servant of his soul, and he makes his soul subject to God. He knows that he is smaller than the cosmos, but he refuses to be intimidated by it, knowing that he is bigger" than the cosmos because he can get the heavens into his head by understanding its laws. That leaves him one supreme task: To get his head into the heavens. On this human level, man knows that he came from God and that to God he must return. Hence the universe is to be viewed sacramentally as a material thing to be used for the purpose of leading the good life.

The Divine Level

Living on the human level is not very satisfactory, not only because reason is limited, and the will weak, but also because, on this human level, our relations to God are not clear.

As it is possible for man to sink below the human level, so it is also possible for him to be raised above it. This he cannot do by his own power. A crystal cannot become a flower, nor can man become a child of God by his own unaided effort. No moral effort, no evolutionary process, no intensification of philanthropy can lift man to the spiritual level by which he participates in the Life of God.

The plant cannot live in the animal unless the animal takes it up into its kingdom. In a more rigid way, man cannot live in God and share His Divine Life unless the Divine Life comes down and lifts him up to its level. One cannot live a human life unless born to it, and one cannot live a divine life unless born to it. Between the human and the divine level there is a law on guard: The law that life comes from life, and God-life comes from God. "Amen, amen I say to thee, unless a man be born again of water and the Holy Ghost, he cannot enter into the kingdom of God." (John 3:5) This birth on the divine level is the Sacrament of Baptism.

By being "born again" of the spirit and not of the flesh, we are lifted to the *super*-natural level, one to which we are no more entitled by nature than a rose is entitled to hearing, or a dog is entitled to speech. Naturally, we are creatures of God; supernaturally, we are children of God. In the natural order, God is Creator, Providence, or the End of man. In the supernatural order, God the Father is our Creator, God the Son our Redeemer, and God the Holy Spirit our Sanctifier.

This mystical unity with God, which is born in our soul in Baptism, is actualized by Faith, Hope, and Charity, and is increased by gifts of the Holy Spirit and the Sacraments. Thus it is evident that though union with God is a free gift, it cannot be preserved nor increased *without our cooperation.* I might wake up some morning and discover I had suddenly been infused with the gift of playing the piano; but unless I practiced from that point on, I could lose the gift. Similarly, the gift of faith must not be left barren.

There are ultimately only two possible theories to account for the nature and the origin of man: One is that the life of man is a push from below; the other, that the life of man is a gift from above. The one is that man is wholly of the earth earthly; the other that he is partly of the heaven heavenly. The second is the Christian conception: man is not a risen beast, he is rather a kind of fallen angel. His origin is hidden not in the slime and dust of prehistoric forests, but in the clear daylight of Paradise where he communed with God; his origin goes back not to cosmic forces, but to divine grace. According to this conception, man is supposed to act not like a beast because he came from one, but like God, because he is made to His own image and likeness.

Which of these two views of man is nobler? The one which regards him as a little biochemical entity of flesh and blood, only about six feet tall, apt to be killed by a microbe, standing self-poised and self-centered in such a universe as this, acknowledging in self-conceit no God, no purpose, no future, and still hoping that the blind cosmic forces of space and time will sweep him on until he becomes lost in the bursting of the great cosmic bubble? Or the other view which shows us that same being awakened to his own actual sinfulness, his possible saintliness; his own actual humanity, his possible sharing in the life of Christ; his enrolling himself, by an act of self-distrust, which is the highest kind of self-assertion, under no less a person than the Son of God, made man, and crying out directly to the Lord of the universe, "I am thine, O God. O help me whom Thou hast made."

When a man answers this question correctly, he will understand something of the true nature of man and the love of God who came to restore the gifts which man had lost, and in gratitude, his heart will cry out: "My God! My God! What is a heart, that

Thou shouldst it so eye, and woo, pouring upon it all Thy art, as if Thou hadst nothing else to do?"

After Christ's ascension into Heaven, how did this Fountainhead of Divine Life communicate that Life to man? He communicated it in the same way He communicated His Truth, and His Power, namely, through His Mystical Body, the Church. Since He had chosen a human nature as the instrument for the sanctification of men during His historical life, so would He use a corporation of human natures as the instrument for the sanctification of men until the end of time.

Just as the invisible energy of my brain descends into all parts of my body, giving movements to arms and legs, muscles and sinews, so there descend beams of grace from the glorified Christ to the members of His Mystical Body. He even went so far as to determine the precise manner in which He would sanctify souls in His Mystical Body, the Church; namely, through the Sacraments.

What is a sacrament?

In the broad sense, a sacrament is a material, visible thing used as a channel for the spiritual and the invisible. The world is made up of sacraments of the natural order. A handshake is a sacrament, in the sense that it is a visible clasping of hands to express the invisible; namely, welcome and friendship.

BAPTISM

How many Sacraments has Christ chosen to vivify His Mystical Body? Since the supernatural life is modeled upon human life, we might expect the number to be seven, and such it actually is. But why seven? Because there are seven conditions upon which life is possible; five which condition our individual life, and two which condition our social life.

In the individual order, the first condition of all life is birth, for obviously unless I am born, I cannot live. In the supernatural order, too, unless I am born to

Christ, I cannot live His life — and this is the Sacrament of Baptism.

CONFIRMATION

Secondly, in the natural order, a man must not only be born but he must also grow from infancy to maturity. In the supernatural order, a soul must grow to spiritual maturity as a perfect cell in the Mystical Body, so that it may overcome obstacles which stand in the way of that divine life — and this is the Sacrament of Confirmation.

THE EUCHARIST

Thirdly, in order to live naturally, a life must nourish itself. In the supernatural order, a soul must nourish the divine life already within it — and this is the Sacrament of the Eucharist.

PENANCE

Fourthly, in the natural order, it sometimes happens that a part of the body may become injured, in which case the wound must be bound and healed. In the supernatural order, it sometimes happens that a soul may sin, in which instance a member of the Mystical Body becomes wounded, or even dies. The spiritual wound must be healed and the inanimate member revivified — and this is the Sacrament of Penance.

EXTREME UNCTION

Fifthly, the last condition of individual life in the natural order is the overcoming of the effects of disease, for a body may not only be wounded, it may suffer from the physical weakness which follows a disease. In the supernatural order, the soul must be freed from the remains of sin, or the moral weakness which comes in the wake of sin- and this is the Sacrament of Extreme Unction.

MATRIMONY

Now to pass to the two other conditions of life which affect us as social beings — for we are not only individuals but also members of society. In the natural order, society is conditioned upon the procreation of our species. In the supernatural order, too, the growth of the Mystical Body is conditioned upon the raising up of children of God — and this is through the Sacrament of Matrimony.

HOLY ORDERS

Finally, as a social being, man must also be governed. This implies officials whose business it is to apply the fruits of law and order to their neighbors. In the supernatural order, too, the members of the Mystical Body must also be governed. This implies ministers in order that the effects of the Redemption may be applied to souls — this is through the Sacrament of Holy Orders.

LIVING WITH GOD

The seven Sacraments are thus channels through which Christ in Heaven builds up His Mystical Body on earth by the infusion of His Divine Life. They are the bridges between Christians and Christ in His Glory; the channels through which the waters of everlasting life pour forth into the garden of the soul. The Sacraments are the kisses of God under the visible sign of which He floods the soul with the riches of His Love.

"What effect can a little water have which is poured on the head of a child? Judge not the existence of those divine outpourings by the matter you see in the Sacraments, which are but the sign of the life within; judge not Baptism by the water, or the Eucharist by the bread, any more than you judge the joy of friendship by a handshake or an embrace.

What is the spoken word but soundwaves put in movement? But when the soul is in it, it becomes eloquence, justice, truth, courage to do and die! Think, then, of what a word is when God puts *His Soul* into it!

What is water but a union of hydrogen and oxygen? Put the genius of man into it and it becomes vapor, commerce, power, civilization. Think then what water is when God puts Himself into it!

What is bread but the mere chemical combination of wheat, water, and yeast? Unite it with the soul of man, and it becomes food, strength, life, joy. Think then of what bread is when God unites His Life with it!

And with the other sacraments; that which strikes the eye in them is weak and poor, but that which strikes the soul is divine.

The Sacraments are the normal channels by which the divine life is poured into our souls. Once we are made "partakers of the divine nature," God becomes present to us in a new way. He is present not only in the universe by His Power, His Wisdom, and His Goodness. He is present not only in the tabernacle where

He dwells in His Body and Blood, Soul and Divinity, under the form of bread; but He is also present in the soul. What causes God to be there? Grace. What can expel Him from there? Sin.

What does this Presence of God in our souls by grace make us? Three things:

A temple of God

"If any one love me, he will keep my word, and my Father will love him, and we will come to him, and will make our abode with him." (John 14:23) "Know you not, that you are the temple of God, and that the Spirit of God dwelleth in you?" (1 Cor. 3:16)

Another Christ by participation

"And I live, now not I; but Christ liveth in me. And that I live now in the flesh: I live in the faith of the Son of God, who loved me, and delivered himself for me." (Gal. 2: 20)

Adopted sons of God

Jesus Christ is the natural Son of God made man. We are only the adopted sons. But because we are sons we have a right to be fed: "Father, give us this day our daily bread." Because we are sons, we have a right to the Father's indulgence: "Father, forgive us our trespasses." Because we are sons, we are heirs of the Kingdom of Heaven. If therefore we are in the state of grace, or possess that similitude to the divine nature, Our Lord will say to us at death: "Come, ye blessed of my Father, possess you the kingdom prepared for you from the foundation of the world." (Matt. 25: 34)

How did we acquire the right to be lifted from the human level of creatures to the superhuman level of children of God? Through the love of the Father who from all eternity chose us and predestined us to be conformable to the image of His Son. Through the love of the Son who, becoming man and dying for us on Calvary, broke down the wall of sin which divided us from God and re- deemed us by His death on the Cross: "In whom we have redemption through his blood, the remission of sins, according to the riches of his grace." (Eph. 1:7) Through the love of the Holy Spirit, who incorporated us to Christ in Baptism: "And such some of you were; but you are washed, but you are sanctified, but you are justified in the name of our Lord Jesus Christ, and the Spirit of our God." (1 Cor. 6:11)

Why is sin wrong?

Because sin is a divorce of man from the Divine Life in the soul. What death is to the body, that sin is to the soul. *Divine Friendship* "For the wages of sin is death." (Rom. 6:23) Man in the state of grace has a double "life." The life of the body is the soul; the life of the soul is grace. When the soul leaves the body, the body dies. When grace leaves the soul, the soul dies. This is a "double death." That is why the greatest tragedy in the world is to die in the state of sin.

Renunciation

Why must the Christian renounce himself by mortification and penance? Original sin was destroyed in our soul by Baptism, but the possibility of actual sin continues. Death is a masterpiece, and no masterpiece was ever made in a day. If therefore we are to die well, that is, in the love of God — we must learn to "die" often during life by renouncing all those things which might injure the love of God in our souls.

Since I am one with Christ by grace, what ought to be my disposition of soul? A constant desire to put on the mind of Christ so that I think about things from "His point of view/' so that I will the things which He wills. Before doing any deed I should ask: 'Will this be pleasing to God?" As Saint Elizabeth of the Trinity said: "We must become an additional humanity for Christ," that is, so putting ourselves at the disposal of Our Lord that He may work through us, as His Sacred Humanity was always at the disposal of the Word.

Glory to God

At what moment do Catholics render most glory to God? In the Holy Sacrifice of the Mass. For no man can glorify God as He deserves, except Our Lord because He is the Son of God and the Son of Man. Therefore, He is the Mediator between God and man. The only true worship of God is through Christ, and it is in the Mass that Jesus Christ is offered to the Father — but not Jesus Christ alone. We are with Him. The work of the Saviour is sufficient only for him who completes it on his own account. In the Mass, we unite ourselves *to* the offering Christ made of Himself upon the Cross. When He died on the Cross we died with Him. "For the charity of Christ presseth us; judging this, that if one died for all, then all were dead." (2 Cor. 5: 14)

For this mystical renewal of Christ's Death in the Mass to take place effectually in each of us, we must unite ourselves to it. And how are we *to* become victims with this Supreme Victim? By yielding ourselves, like Him, to the entire accomplishment of the Divine Will. We must be in the essential attitude of giving *all* to God, of so uniting our mortifications, penances, and trials to His, that we may be able to say as Our Lord did the eve of His Passion: "But that the world may know, that I love the Father: and as the Father hath given me commandment, so do I: Arise, let us go hence" (John 14:31) — that is, to Calvary.

WAYS OF PRESERVING FRIENDSHIPS

We can never be a true friend of anyone whom we do not know. Few of us really know ourselves, and few ever want to know. We imagine ourselves to be very different from what we are. We wear a mask in public but seldom take it off when we are alone. Hence we think that our critics *always* misjudge us. We believe our friends are right when they praise us, and wrong when they criticize us. Most of our acquaintances could tell us faults about ourselves which we would deny most vociferously, and yet they might be only too true.

Know Thyself

For a good reason, therefore, the Greeks inscribed on the Temple of Apollo at Delphi, the injunction: "Know thyself." Plutarch added: "If the 'Know thyself' of the oracle were an easy thing for every man, it would not be held to be a divine injunction."

The Divine Saviour in telling the story of the Prodigal Son marked the moment of the latter's conversion with the words: "Returning to himself, he said," etc. (Luke 15:17)

Self-knowledge is not intellectual, but moral. It falls not within the domain of psychology, but theology; but theology; it is concerned not with what we think, but with our motives and the hidden springs of life and action.

Self-examination must be done in the presence of God — we must compare ourselves *not* with our *neighbor,* nor with our own subjective ideals, but with the Perfect. How often in life we stand self-revealed by coming in contact with a noble life. In self-examination, it is God and not man who makes us enter into ourselves. As Simeon said when he held the Babe: "This *child* is set . . . that out of many hearts, thoughts may be revealed." (Luke 2: *34, 35*)

In that wondrous Presence, there can be room neither for hidden pride nor barren hopelessness.

Bewilderment

The neurotic, the bewildered, and the disillusioned are today flocking to psychoanalysts to have their minds analyzed, when what they really need is to go to God to have their sins forgiven.

There can be no health of soul or body while there is a moral conflict within. The modem mind thought it got rid of hell but found it within. A psychoanalyst can sublimate; God alone can give peace.

As Dr. Jung, the celebrated psychoanalyst, admitted: "About a third of my cases are suffering from no clinically definable neurosis, but from the senselessness and emptiness of their lives. This can be described as the general neurosis of our time. A considerable number of patients came to see me, not because they were suffering from neuroses, but because they were finding no meaning in life"

Lives are disordered and unhappy because they are *multiple.* Like broken mirrors, they reflect a hundred different objects, but no single purpose which could give unity to life. Our Lord asked the name of the devil who possessed the soul of the young man, and the devil answered: "Legion." He had lost his unity.

One of the reasons of this tension *within* is because we have never settled absolutely for ourselves whether our body or our soul should dominate. If we concentrate on the pleasures of the body, we surrender the joys of the soul. If we concentrate on the soul, we make the body its servant, and therefore a sharer in the joys of the soul. So long as we are without a goal of living, we are like a radio tuned in to two different stations, getting no harmony but only static, no enjoyment but only a feeling of irritation.

Goal of living

What is the goal of human living? That question has already been answered: To attain Perfect Life without death, Truth without error, and Love without hate or satiety — which is God.

A man is happy when he fulfills the end for which he is made. Creatures of all kinds — gold, food, machinery, flesh, money are means to attain God. It is making them the *ends* of life which constitutes selfishness and causes sin and disorder. This comes so easily to our fallen natures, that we must constantly be on our guard. To this end, a self-examination should be made every night before retiring and should be followed by a prayer expressing sorrow for our sins, asking God for forgiveness, and resolving to amend our ways and to do penance for the sins we have committed.

This examination can be very brief. It should revolve around the seven capital sins, the seven pallbearers of the soul:

Pride

Pride is an inordinate love of one's own excellence and, as such, it dethrones God from the soul and enthrones "I". "No God, no Master. I am God. I am my own Lord." Every proud person takes himself too seriously.

Human beings are like sponges. Each human being can stand so much honor, as a sponge can hold so much water. Both quickly reach a point of saturation. When a sponge passes that point, it drips; when a man passes that point, the honor wears him instead of him wearing the honor.

The proud person exaggerates his own personal qualities, talks about himself, his accomplishments, is jealous of everyone else — as if others, by gaining an honor, had stolen it from him. Associated with this is constant fault-finding.

The envious never know that their criticism of others is vicarious self-criticism. The man who accuses another of infidelity, jealousy, or pride is generally guilty of those sins himself. Thus he projects to others his own faults and is judged in his judgment of others.

Have I attributed to my own judgment a higher value than the wisdom of God, or His Moral Law, or the Christian tradition, or the teaching of His Church?

Have I presumed to pass judgment on religious doctrines which I hardly understood?

Have I drawn others into sin by sneering that God's law was out of date, or was impossible, or old-fashioned?

How can God fill me with His grace if I am already filled with self?

Do I realize that any talents or gifts I have received came from God, and therefore I ought to thank Him? "For who distinguisheth thee? Or what hast thou that thou hast not received? And if thou hast received, why dost thou glory, as if thou hadst not received *it?*" (1 Cor. 4:7)

Do I always seek to be seen? Do I seek notoriety or publicity as if the be-all and end-all of life were to be known by men? "But when thou are invited, go, sit down in the lowest place; that when he who invited thee, cometh, he may say *to* thee: Friend, go up higher. Then shalt thou have glory before them that sit at table with thee." (Luke 14:10)

Do I ever practice humility or recognize the truth about myself? "Take up my yoke upon you, and learn of me, because I am meek, and humble of heart: And you shall find rest to your souls." (Matt. 11:29)

Avarice

Avarice is the inordinate love of earthly goods. Undue love of money gives a man a "heart of gold" — cold and yellow.

Do I seek wealth regardless of the rights of others?

Do I spend superfluities only on myself or for my own pleasure; for example, for drink, entertainment, etc., instead of on others, that is, the poor, the sick, or on churches for the poor?

Do I advertise to enlarge my business rather than pay a living wage to my employees?

Have I over a long period of time refused to give alms to the poor, the needy, or the afflicted?

Do I realize that on the day of my death the only possessions I really will have will be those I gave away, for their merit will still be with me?

Have I pondered on the words of Our Lord: "Lay not up to yourselves treasures on earth: where the rust and moth consume, and where thieves break through and steal. But lay up to yourselves treasures in heaven: where neither the rust nor moth doth consume, and where thieves do not break through, nor steal." (Matt. 6:19, 20)

"Seek ye therefore first the kingdom of God, and his justice, and all these things shall be added unto you." (Matt. 6:33)

Envy

Envy is discontent with another's good, a mentality which is cast down at another's good, as if it were an affront to our own superiority.

Do I assert my envy by "running down" others by innuendo, half-truths, fault-finding, or by attributing to them false motives?

Have I rejoiced over the misfortunes of others?

Have I ever tried to cure my jealousy by praying for the one of whom I was jealous?

Why have I not made the quality of a neighbor an occasion for imitation rather than envy, and thus increased in some way the welfare of humanity and the glory of God: "But if you bite and devour one another: take heed you be not consumed one of another." (Gal. 5:15)

Is my sympathy for the needy inspired by love of the poor or by hatred of the rich?

Anger

Unjust anger is a violent and inordinate desire to punish others, and is often accompanied by hatred which seeks not only to repel aggression, but to take revenge.

Am I impatient with others? Do I *buy* into "fits of temper" and make cutting and sarcastic remarks because my will has been crossed?

Do I find excuses for being provoked at my neighbor, but never admit the same excuse for him being provoked at me?

Do I ever practice patience, that is, think before I speak, then talk to myself?

Have I ever asked myself how will God forgive my sins if I do not forgive the faults of others?

Do I realize that being quickly aroused to anger is a sign of selfishness, and that my character is known from the things I hate? If I love God, I will hate sin; if I love sin, I will hate religion. "Judge not that you may not be judged." (Matt. 7:1)

Gluttony

Gluttony is the abuse of the lawful pleasure God has attached to eating and drinking, which are necessary conditions of self-preservation. It becomes sinful when it incapacitates us for the fulfillment of our duties, injures our health, endangers the interests of others, or when — for Catholics — it breaks the laws of fast and abstinence.

Have I made others suffer as a result of intoxication? Have I, a Catholic, broken the laws of the Church concerning fast and abstinence?

Have I encouraged others to drink more than was good for them?

Do I advert to the fact that the principal danger of the "Cocktail hour" and frequentation of bars is not complete intoxication, but the materialization of life and the loss of spiritual values?

Do I appreciate that God's gifts of food and drink and other necessities are *means,* not ends; that is, that they are given for the renewal of my strength, that I might place myself in His service? 'Therefore, whether you eat or drink, or whatsoever else you do, do all to the glory of God." (1 Cor. 10:31)

Sloth

Sloth is a malady of the will which causes us to neglect our duties. It is physical sloth when it manifests itself in laziness, procrastination, idleness, and indifference. It is spiritual sloth when it shows a distaste for the things of the spirit, a hurrying of devotions, a religious lukewarmness, and a failure to cultivate new virtues.

Do I accept ready-made opinions from propagandists, instead of thinking them out for myself in the perspective of history and ethics?

Do I excuse myself from taking Christianity seriously on some such ill-considered ground as that the Christ-life is unacceptable to twentieth-century standards?

Do I do any serious reading to improve my spiritual condition?

Have I been neglectful of my duties to God?

Do I pray?

"And withal being idle, they learn to go about from house to house: and are not only idle, but tattlers also, and busybodies, speaking things which they ought not." (Tim. 5:13)

Lust

Lust is an inordinate love of the pleasures of the flesh. God attached pleasure to eating and drinking that the individual life might be preserved; He also attached great pleasure to the marital act in order that social life and the Kingdom of God might be preserved.

The pleasure becomes sinful when used as an exclusive end rather than a means. Lust, for that reason, is perverted love. It looks not to the good of the other, but to the pleasure of self. It breaks the glass that holds the wine, and smashes the lute to snare the music.

Have I consented to evil thoughts?

If it is wrong to do a certain thing, must I not also refuse to think about that thing? "Whosoever shall look on a woman to lust after her, hath already committed adultery with her in his heart." (Matt. 5:28)

Have I encouraged others to sin by thought, word, or deed?

Have I violated purity by thought, word, or deed? Have I tried to cultivate a higher love, and thus sublimate a lower?

Honesty is a burden only to those who have lost the sense of others' rights, and purity a burden for the same reason.

"Know you not, that you are the temple of God, and that the spirit of God dwelleth in you?" (1 Cor. 3:16)

"All things are clean to the clean: but to them that are
defiled, and to unbelievers, nothing is clean: but both their mind and their conscience are defiled." (Titus 1:15)

"Dearly beloved, I beseech you as strangers and pilgrims, to refrain yourselves from carnal desires which war against the soul." (1 Pet. 2:11)

"I beseech you therefore, brethren, by the mercy of God, that you present your bodies a living sacrifice, holy, pleasing unto God, your reasonable service." (Rom. 12:1)

"Blessed are the clean of heart: for they shall see God." (Matt. 5:8)

DISCIPLINING MYSELF FOR LOVE

I am a child of God

We become children of God and heirs of Heaven by being "re-born" in the Sacrament of Baptism. But to proceed from this ordinary unconscious union of grace to an ever-growing union of will requires, among other things, a certain amount of self-discipline. In order that the spirit may not be in bondage to the flesh, the flesh must be subdued, without ever annihilating it or destroying our nature.

Self-discipline may be defined as a struggle against evil inclinations in order to subject them to our own will and ultimately to the will of God.

The modem world is opposed to self-discipline on the ground that personality must be "self-expressive." Self-expression is right so long as it does not end in self-destruction. A boiler that would be self-expressive by blowing up, or an engine that would be self-expressive by jumping the tracks, would both be acting contrary to their natures as fashioned by the minds of the engineers who designed them. So, too, if man acts contrary to what is best and highest in his nature by rebelling against the Eternal Reason of God, his Creator, his self-expression is self-destruction.

We have a body and we have a soul. Each has different satisfactions; the pleasures of one militate against the pleasures of the other. Each has a different landing field. Tension, neurosis, and unhappiness come from the attempt to satisfy both. "No man can serve two masters." (Matt. 6:24) "For he that will save his life, shall lose it: and he that shall lose his life for my sake, shall find it." (Matt. 16:25)

The condition of being a true Christian is to be self-disciplined. "If any man will come after me, let him deny himself, and take up his cross daily, and follow me." (Luke 9:23) "For if you live according to the flesh, you shall die: but if by the Spirit you mortify the deeds of the flesh, you shall live." (Rom. 8:13) "And they that are Christ's, have crucified their flesh, with the vices and concupiscences."

(Gal. 5:24) So "if thy right eye scandalize thee, pluck it out and cast it from thee. For it is expedient for thee that one of thy members should perish, rather than thy whole body be cast into hell." (Matt. 5:29)

Love

Love is the inspiration of all sacrifice. Love is not the desire to have, to own, to possess — that is selfishness. Love is the desire to be had, to be owned, to be possessed. It is the giving of oneself for another.

The symbol of love, as the world understands it, is the circle continually surrounded by self, thinking only of self. The symbol of love, as Christ understands it, is the Cross with its arms outstretched even unto eternity to embrace all souls within its grasp.

Sinful love, as the world understands it, finds its type in Judas the night of the betrayal: "What will you give me and I will deliver him unto you." (Matt. 26:15) Love in its true sense finds its type in Christ a few hours later when, mindful of his disciples, He says to the friends of the traitor who blistered His lips with a kiss, "If therefore you seek me, let these go their way." (John 18:8)

Love is the giving of self. So long as we have a body and are working out our salvation, love will always be synonymous with sacrifice, in the Christian sense of the word.

Love sacrifices naturally, just as the eye sees naturally and the ear hears naturally. That is why we speak of "arrows" and "darts" of love — something that wounds.

The bridegroom who loves will not give to his bride a ring of tin or of brass, but the best he can obtain — platinum, if he can afford it, because the gold or platinum ring represents sacrifice; it costs something.

The mother who sits up all night nursing her sick child does not call it hardship, but love.

The day men forget that love is synonymous with sacrifice, they will ask, What a selfish sort of woman it must be who ruthlessly extracts tribute in the form of flowers, just as they do ask, What cruel kind of God is it who asks for sacrifice and self-denial? Love is the reason of all immolation.

Hence the man who loves his perfected life in Christ, will die to himself — and this dying to himself, this taming of his members as so many wild beasts, this being imprinted with the Cross, is mortification.

DISCIPLINE

Keep the imagination under control. You can imagine a mountain of gold, but you will never own one. The imagination promises what it can never deliver on this earth.

Know how to refuse. By consenting to every common impulse and the pleasure of every sense, one becomes a

"Yes-man" to the voice of self-destruction. Our character is made by our choices.

The purpose of discipline is charity. Mortification is a means to the love of God and neighbor, and not an end in itself. The gifts of God are our servants. It is when they become rebel servants, or our masters, that we need to tame them.

In self-discipline, you "give up" nothing. You merely "exchange." You find that you can get along without an excess of drink, but you cannot give up peace of mind or union with God so you "exchange" one for another. "What exchange shall a man give for his soul?" (Matt. 16:26)

Our heart adheres the more intimately to one thing, the more it withdraws from others. That is why we close our eyes when we wish to concentrate. That is why in the higher regions of religion, consecrated souls leave the world to give themselves to the first love which is the Last Love — God.

The purpose of self-discipline is to build a hierarchy. Senses are made subservient to reason, reason to faith, body to soul, and man to God.

Self-discipline requires patience. Since we do not acquire evil habits in a day, we will not break them in a day. The abuses of years may take years to rectify. "If any man will come after me, let him deny himself, and take up his cross daily, and follow me." (Luke 9:23)

The soul is made by what gets into it. Just as health depends on what we eat, so the holiness of mind depends on what we think. As we avoid poisons for the sake of the body, so we avoid evil thoughts, conversations, books, magazines, motion pictures, and companionships for the sake of the soul.

We should never let a day pass without doing three small mortifications, for example, not taking that extra cigarette or that second lump of sugar. Thus do we possess ourselves instead of being possessed by things. When these mortifications are done in the name of Our Lord, they become a source of great merit as well.

We will find God to the degree that we renounce ourselves.

Some tests of knowing our nearness to God are: The patient and uncomplaining bearing of the slights and crosses of daily life; an even temper and a cheerfulness of spirit even under trying circumstances; the undertaking of all duties and legitimate pleasures and actions in the name of God and for the glory of God; a greater readiness to serve those who cannot profit us, rather than those who can.

Some motives for self-discipline are: To obtain peace of soul; to atone for one's sins; to obtain some favor or grace; to live a life more intimately with God; to conform oneself to Christ-suffering; to make reparation for the sins of others.

LOVE OF NEIGHBOR
IN GENERAL

There are three kinds of love. There is instinctive love, which we have in common with animals. Human beings experience it when they love not the person, but the pleasure which the person gives. The modern world calls this "sex."

The second kind of love is the distinctly human love of self-disinterestedness, which springs from an appreciation of the beauty or goodness of human nature when seen at its best. In instinctive love the good is horizontal — it refers to a good on the *same plane.*

The human love of disinterestedness is, on the contrary, vertical — it looks to a goodness on a higher plane, but still within the category of the human. It is more abstract than concrete. For example, the Philanthropist love "humanity," the Communist his "class," the Nazi his "race", and the Fascist his "nation," the Revolutionist his "cause," the soldier his "country", etc.

In each case, there is a love for an abstract "good," without any explicit reference to the source and standard of Goodness.

The third kind of love is not limited either by self-disinterestedness, nor by a high form of human goodness, but derives its inspiration from the unlimited self-giving of Divine Love which found its highest expression in Christ who died for sinners. His death was not a superlative revelation of human love, but an infinite manifestation of Divine Love; for God "spared not even his own Son." (Rom. 8:32)

Not many of us understand this third form of love because, being shut up in the circle of narrow self-interest, we can see no further than self-interest allows. We can love those who love us, and we can do good to those who do good to us, but a God who is "kind to the unthankful, and to the evil" (Luke 6:35), we fail to comprehend.

By combining the first two forms of love, one may speak of a double inspiration for fellowship. One, natural, and based on particular mutual affinities or interests — for such motives men form lodges, unions, and other organizations. The other, supernatural or divine, forbidding the claim of personal characteristics or class interests to count for anything. We are to love our fellowman not because he is lovable but because God loves him.

Brotherhood

It should be evident that the sharing of economic wealth will not make us brothers, but becoming brothers will make us share our economic wealth. The early Christians were not one because they pooled their wealth; they pooled their wealth because they were Christians.

The rich young man went to Our Lord asking: "What shall I do?" The Socialist asks: "What will *society* do?" It is man who makes society and not society which makes man. That is why all the economic schemes from Marx's Communism to the latest form of Democratic Collectivism will never unite men until they have first learned to burn, purge and cut away their own selfishness.

The "One World" will not come at the end of an ascending line of progress, but as the Resurrection from a tomb of a thousand crucified egotisms.

The reason Christianity lives and Socialist theories perish is because Socialism makes no provision for getting rid of selfishness, but Our Lord did: "Sell all whatever thou hast, and give to the poor." (Luke 18:22)

The only place in the world where communism works is in a convent, for there the basis of having everything in common is that no one wants anything. Communism has not worked in Moscow, but it does work in a monastery.

All that economic and political revolutions do is to shift booty and loot from one party's packet to another. For that reason, none of them is really revolutionary: they all leave greed in the heart of man.

The true inspiration for fellowship is not law but love. Law is negative: "Thou shalt *not.*" Love is positive: *"Love* God and *love* neighbor." Law is concerned with the minimum: "Speed limit, 35 miles." Love is concerned with the maximum: "Be ye perfect as your heavenly Father is perfect."

Law is for moderation; love is generous: "And if a man will contend with thee in judgment, and take away thy coat, let go thy cloak also unto him. And whosoever will force thee one mile, go with him other two." (Matt. 5: 40-41)

Natural generosity is limited by circumstances and relations within our own circle, and outside of these is often vindictive. Love ignores all limits, by forgiveness.

"Lord, how often shall my brother offend against me, and I forgive him? till seven times? ... I say not to thee, till seven times; but till seventy times seven times." (Matt. 18:21-22) By moving from a little metaphor to a big one, Our Lord implies that precision in forgiveness is impossible.

Leave it to love and it is not likely to err on the lower side.

The love of which we speak is not natural, but supernatural. By faith and good works under God's grace, nourished by prayer and the Sacraments, we are led into intimate union with Christ — but this love we have toward Him must redound to all His creatures.

Supernatural Love

After instituting the Holy Eucharist, the night before He died, Our Lord revealed the secrets of His Heart by giving what he called a *new commandment.* "A new commandment I give unto you: That you love one another, as I have loved you, that you also love one another." (John 13:34)

Why was this precept of *charity* (for that is the proper term to describe supernatural love) — why was this precept new? Because the explicit command to love all men, regardless of race or class, or color, even though they be enemies, had never been affirmed before. From that time on, the one mark by which His followers would be known would be their supernatural love for all. "By this shall all men know that you are my disciples, if you have love one for another." (John 13:35)

On the last day when He will come to render to every man according to his works, it will be by charity to God and to fellowman that salvation will be decided. Until the consummation of time, Christ will move through the world hidden under the guise of the needy, the poor, and the oppressed.

"Then shall the king say to them that shall be on his right hand: Come, ye blessed of my Father, possess you the kingdom prepared for you from the foundation of the world. For I was hungry, and you gave me to eat: I was thirsty, and you gave me to drink: I was a stranger, and you took me in: naked, and you covered me; sick, and you visited me: I was in prison, and you came to me.

"Then shall the just answer him, saying: Lord, when did we see thee hungry, and fed thee; thirsty, and gave thee drink? And when did we see thee a stranger and took thee in? Or naked, and covered thee? Or when did we see you sick or in prison, and came to thee? And the king answering, shall say to them: Amen I say to you, as long as you did it to one of these my least brethren, you did it to me.

"Then he shall say to them also that shall be on his left hand: Depart from me, you cursed, into everlasting fire which was prepared for the devil and his angels. For I was hungry, and you gave me not to eat: I was thirsty, and you gave me not to drink: I was a stranger, and you took me not in: naked and you covered me not: sick and in prison, and you did not visit me.

"Then they also shall answer him, saying: Lord, when did we see thee hungry, or thirsty, or a stranger, or naked, or sick, or in prison, and did not minister to thee?

"Then he shall answer them, saying: Amen I say to you, as long as you did it not to one of these least, neither did you do it to me. And these shall go into everlasting punishment: but the just, into life everlasting." (Matt. 25:34-46)

One of the tests of our love of God is our love of neighbor, for it is certain that we will never love our neighbor perfectly unless we love God perfectly.

It is so easy to love those of our circle, but to love those who are "below" us, or opposed to us, or "ignorant," or apparently not "worth our time," requires true spiritual insight.

"For if you love them that love you, what reward shall you have? do not even the publicans this? And if you salute your brethren only, what do you more? do not also the heathens this? Be you, therefore, perfect, as also your heavenly Father is perfect." (Matt. 5:46-48)

God's attitude towards us is regulated by our attitude towards our neighbor. That is why if we need something badly, the best way to *pray* for it is to give something away. If we have sinned and need forgiveness, then let us forgive our

117

enemies. God will never be outdone by our love.

"For with what judgment you judge, you shall be judged: and with what measure you mete, it shall be measured to you again." (Matt. 7:2)

"Give and it shall be given to you: good measure and pressed down and shaken together and running over shall they give into your bosom. For with the same measure that you shall mete withal, it shall be measured to you again." (Luke 6:38)

Charity

St. Paul reminds us that charity is superior to eloquence, to prophecy, to philanthropy, to humanistic martyrdom. "If I speak with the tongues of men, and of angels, and have not charity, I am become as sounding brass, or tinkling cymbal. And if I should have prophecy and should know all mysteries, and all knowledge, and if I should have all faith, so that I could remove mountains, and have not charity, I am nothing. And if I should distribute all my goods to feed the poor, and if I should deliver my body to be burned, and have not charity, it profiteth me nothing." (1 Cor. 13:1-3)

Charity is greater than faith, for in heaven there will be no faith. How can one merely "believe" when one actually "sees"?

Charity is greater than hope, for there will be no hope in heaven. How can one hope when one possesses?

But there will be charity; for God is love. "And now there remain faith, hope, and charity, these three: but the greatest of these is charity." (1 Cor. 13:13)

There are nine ingredients to charity: "Charity is patient, is kind: charity envieth not, dealeth not perversely; is not puffed up; Is not ambitious, seeketh not her own, is not provoked to anger, thinketh no evil; Rejoiceth not in iniquity, but rejoiceth with the truth." (1 Cor. 13:4-6)

Patience

"Charity is patient." Charity is never in a hurry; it knocks, but breaks down no doors. A charitable heart, like the Church, knows that evil is transitory. Though evil has its "hour" as it did in the Garden of Gethsemane, God will have His "day." "But that on the good ground, are they who in a good and perfect heart, hearing the word, keep it, and bring forth fruit in patience." (Luke 8:15) "In your patience, you shall possess your souls." (Luke 21:19)

"Be patient, therefore, brethren, until the coming of the Lord. Behold, the husbandman waiteth for the precious fruit of the earth: patiently bearing till he receive the early and latter *rain*. Be you therefore also patient, and strengthen your hearts: for the coming of the Lord is at hand. Behold, we account them blessed who have endured. You have heard of the patience of Job, and you have seen the end of the Lord, that the Lord is merciful and compassionate. (James 5:7, 8, 11)

Kindness

"Charity ... is kind." The whole life of Our Lord has been summarized thus: "He went about doing good." No soul ever saves itself in isolation. We pray in the context of *"Our* Father," and live in the solidarity of the "Mystical Body of Christ." Charity is emancipation from selfishness; it is a going outside of self for the interests of others.

Although it is *kindness,* the essence of love is not *feeling.*

"My son, in thy good deeds, make no complaint, and when thou givest any thing, add not grief by an evil word." (Sirach 18:15) "And be ye kind one *to* another; merciful, forgiving one another, even as God hath forgiven you in Christ." (Eph. 4:32)

Generosity

"Charity envieth not." Jealousy and envy are the tributes which mediocrity pays to genius. Charity is never competitive; it always goes beyond the limits of service or measure. When we rest on the laurels of the ordinary, we clip the wings of charity.

True generosity never looks to reciprocity; it gives neither because it expects a gift in return, nor because there is a duty or obligation to give. Charity lies beyond obligation; its essence is the "adorable extra." Its reward is in the joy of giving.

"When thou makest a dinner or a supper, call not thy friends, nor thy brethren, not thy kinsmen, nor they neighbors who are rich; lest perhaps they also invite thee again, and a recompense be made to thee. But when thou makest a feast, call the poor, the maimed, the lame, and the blind; And thou shalt be blessed, because they have not wherewith to make thee recompense: for recompense shall be made thee at the resurrection of the just." (Luke 14:12-14)

"And if you lend to them of whom you hope to receive, what thanks are to you? For sinners also lend to sinners, for to receive as much. But love ye your enemies: do good and lend, hoping for nothing thereby: and your reward shall be great, and you shall be the sons of the Highest; for he is kind to the unthankful, and to the evil. Be ye therefore merciful, as your Father also is merciful." (Luke 6:34-36)

Humility

"Charity is not pretentious, is not puffed up." Humility is *truth*: seeing ourselves as we really *are*; that is, as God knows our hearts. Affectation is cheating; boasting is an admission of our own indigence. Charity hides itself. The greater the vacuum there is in our heart, the more room there is for God. Full of self, empty of God.

"Thou hypocrite, cast out first the beam out of thy own eye, and then shalt thou see to cast out the mote out of thy brother's eye." (Matt. 7:5)

"But when thou art invited to a wedding, sit not down in the first place, lest perhaps one more honourable than thou be invited by him." (Luke 14:8)

"Take up my yoke upon you ... and learn of me, because I am meek, and humble of heart: and you shall find rest to your souls." (Matt. 11:29)

Renunciation

"Charity ... is not ambitious." The poet warned: "I charge thee, fling away ambition. By that sin fell the angels; how can man then, the image of his Maker, hope to win by it."

"There is a rightful pursuit of the best, but what is here condemned is an insatiable lust for glory or wealth or prestige which is purchased by crawling on others' backs."The fire never saith: It is enough." (Prov. 30:16)

"Charity seeks glory, too; not the glory of men, but the glory of God. It is even willing to have its worldly position sacrificed for the advancement of truth and honor. "Blessed are ye when they shall revile you, and persecute you, and speak all that is evil against you, untruly, for my sake." (Matt. 5:11)

"It shall not be so among you, but whosoever will be the greater among you, let him be your minister: And he that will be first among you, shall be your servant." (Matt. 20:26-27)

"The kings of the Gentiles lord it over them; and they that have power over them, are called beneficent. But you not so: but he that is the greater among you, let him become as the younger; and he that is the leader, as he that serveth. For which is greater, he that sitteth at table, or he that serveth? Is not he that sitteth at table? But I am in the midst of you, as he that serveth." (Luke 22:25-27)

"However, many of the chief men also believed in him; but because of the Pharisees, they did not confess *him*, that they might not be cast out of the synagogue. For they loved the glory of men more than the glory of God." (John 12:42-43)

Unselfishness

"Charity . . . seeketh not her own." The way to win friends and influence people is not to flatter them, but to be selfless. The greatest happiness in life comes not from having, but from giving. From the Christian point of view, the true master is the servant.

The selfish soul who says: "I am going to do as I wish" really means "I am going to force others to do as I wish." No one loves himself too little. About the only romance some souls have is the unhappy one of loving only themselves.

The sign of the end of the world will be selfishness. "Know also this, that, in the last days, shall come dangerous times. Men shall be lovers of themselves, covetous, haughty, proud, blasphemers, disobedient to parents, ungrateful, wicked." (2 Tim. 3:1-2)

"But before all things have a constant mutual charity among yourselves: for charity covereth a multitude of sins." (1 Pet. 4:8)

"And that he should be loved with the whole heart, and with the whole understanding, and with the whole soul, and with the whole strength; and to love one's neighbour as one's self, is a greater

thing than all holocausts and sacrifices."
(Mark 12:33)

"See thou never do to another what
thou wouldst hate to have done to thee by
another." (Tobit 4:16)

"Greater love than this no man hath,
that a man lay down his life for his
friends." (John 15:13)

"For God so loved the world, as to give
his only begotten Son; that whosoever
believeth in him, may not perish, but may
have life everlasting." (John 3:16)

"Bear ye one another's burdens; and
so you shall fulfill the law of Christ." (Gal.
6:2)

Good Temper

"Charity ... is not provoked to anger."
Bad temper is an indication of a man's
character; every man can be judged by the
things which make him mad. Heaven could
be ruined by one single soul who was
touchy. "A peaceable tongue is a tree of life:
but that which is immoderate, shall crush

the spirit." (Prov. 15:4) "A hot soul is a burning fire; it will never be quenched, till it devour something." (Sirach 23:22)

The way to sweeten a soul is not just to take hate out, but to put love in. The even-tempered man possesses his soul. He never flies into a rage at others because he knows that God might rightfully be angry with him. By practicing good-naturedness with others, he hopes to obtain the blessing of God on himself.

Our Lord did not throw stones back at those who would have taken His life. "They took up stones therefore to cast at him. But Jesus hid himself, and went out of the temple." (John 8:59)

"A mild answer breaketh wrath, but a harsh word stirreth up fury." (Prov. 15:1)

"Brethren, and if a man be overtaken in any fault, you, who are spiritual, instruct such a one in the spirit of meekness, considering thyself, lest thou also be tempted." (Gal. 6:1)

"But the servant of the Lord must not wrangle: but be mild towards all men, apt to teach, patient." (2 Tim. 2:24)

Guilelessness

"Charity . . . thinketh no evil." Those who most readily attribute evil to others are generally themselves evil. A dishonest politician will invariably accuse all politicians of being dishonest; an unfaithful husband will accuse his wife of infidelity.

The sense of justice is so deep-rooted in us that if we are not good, we try to pacify our consciences by attributing the same evil to others. Charity, on the contrary, is unsuspicious; and, because it believes in others, is most encouraging of good. Charity never imputes the evil motive, never judges solely by externals.

"Whosoever speaketh ill of anything, bindeth himself for the time to come: but he that feareth the commandment, shall dwell in peace." (Prov. 13:13)

"But do not apply thy heart to all words that are spoken: lest perhaps thou hear thy servant reviling thee. For thy conscience knoweth that thou also hast often spoken evil of others." (Ecc. 7:22-23)

"For our glory is this, the testimony of our conscience, that in simplicity of heart and sincerity of God, and not in carnal wisdom, but in the grace of God, we have conversed in this world: and more abundantly towards you." (2 Cor. 1:12)

"Purifying your souls in the obedience of charity, with a brotherly love, from a sincere heart love one another earnestly." (1 Peter 1:22)

"That you may be blameless, and sincere children of God, without reproof, in the midst of a crooked and perverse generation; among whom you shine as lights in the world." (Phil. 2:15)

Sincerity

"Charity rejoiceth not in iniquity, but rejoiceth with the truth." It is a common human standard to judge virtues by the vices from which we abstain; and to find the wickedness of others an excuse for our own: "I am just as good as the next fellow."

Charity, on the contrary, refuses to capitalize on others' failings. Its joy is found in truth, and in things as they really are. Charity refuses to subscribe to the modem dictum that "good and evil depend entirely on your subjective point of view." *In truth,* means independent of self.

"Woe to you that call evil good, and good evil: that put darkness *for* light, and light *for* darkness: that put bitter for sweet, and sweet for bitter." (Isa. 5:20)

"Why art thou seduced, my son, by a strange woman, and art cherished in the bosom of another?" (Prov. 5:20)
"Rejoice in the Lord always; again, I say rejoice." (Phil. 4:4)

"The kingdom of heaven is like unto a treasure hidden in a field. Which a man having found, hid it, and for joy thereof goeth, and selleth all that he hath, and buyeth that field." (Matt. 13:44)

"Delight in the Lord, and he will give thee the requests of thy heart." (Ps. 36:4)

"So also you now indeed have sorrow; but I will see you again, and your heart shall rejoice; and your joy no man shall take from you." (John 16:22)

Physical and spiritual expressions of charity

There are seven ways in which Charity may be expressed physically:

To feed the hungry.
To give drink to the thirsty.
To clothe the naked.
To succor the stranger.
To visit the sick.
To ransom the captive.
To bury the dead.

LOVE OF NEIGHBOR IN GENERAL

There are seven ways in which Charity may be expressed spiritually:

To instruct the ignorant.
To counsel the doubtful.
To admonish sinners.
To bear wrongs patiently.
To forgive offenses willingly.
To comfort the afflicted.
To pray for the living and the dead.

LOVE OF NEIGHBOR IN GENERAL

FRIENDSHIP OF CHRISTIANS WITH JEWS

Our Christian faith is like a grafted branch that grows out from the roots of the Olive Tree of Israel. Shall Christians delay the day of the fellowship of all men in God, by hatred of a people from whom salvation came as from a root?

"For if the first fruit be holy, so is the lump also: and if the root be holy, so are the branches. And if some of the branches be broken, and thou, being a wild olive, art ingrafted in them, and art made partaker of the root, and of the fatness of the olive tree, Boast not against the branches. But if thou boast, thou hearest not the root, but the root thee ... Be not high-minded, but fear. For if God hath not spared the natural branches, fear lest perhaps he also spare not thee." (Rom. 11:16-18; 20-21)

For a Catholic, to be anti-Semitic is to be un-Catholic.

Pope Pius XI, commenting on the words in the Canon of the Mass --

"sacrifricium Patriarchae nostril Ahrahae," the sacrifice of our father Abraham — said, "Notice that Abraham is called our Patriarch, our ancestor. Anti-Semitism is incompatible with the thought and the sublime reality expressed in this text. It is a movement in which we Christians can have no part whatsoever.... Anti-Semitism is unacceptable. Spiritually we are Semites."

There are many lies told against the Jews. One of them is *The Protocols of the Elders of Zion* which inspires so much anti-Semitism. It supposedly contains an elaborate war plan for the attainment of world dominion through Jewish Freemasons' Lodges.

This work is a forgery. It appeared for the first time in a book written by a certain Russian anti-Semite, Sergius Nilius, entitled *The Great and the Small*, which revealed the anti-Christ as a near political possibility.

The fact is Nilius plagiarized these ideas from the work of a French lawyer, Maurice Joly, *Dialogues in Hell*, published in 1865 — with this principal difference:

Joly made Napoleon the one who sought world domination. Nilius changed Napoleon III to the Jews and so the lie was born.

What would Christianity be without Jesus who came to the world from Israel?

What would the Church be without the twelve Jews who were Apostles of the Messiah?

What would Christianity be without the background of Abraham, Moses, Isaac, John the Baptist, and the prophets who announced the Messiah?

Did not Our Lord Himself say: "Do not think that I am come to destroy the law, or the prophets. I am not come to destroy, but to fulfill. For amen, I say unto you, till heaven and earth pass, one jot, or one tittle shall not pass of the law, till all be fulfilled." (Matt. 5:17-18)

Did not Philip cry out to Nathaniel when they saw Jesus: "We have found him of whom Moses in the law, and the prophets did write, Jesus the son of Joseph of Nazareth." (John 1:45)

The promise of a Saviour was made to the Jews, not to the Gentiles.

A Christian may attempt to justify his anti-Semitism on the ground that the Jews are hated by the world. Shall the Christian forget that if he were a real Christian, he, too, would be hated by the world: "I have chosen you out of the world, therefore the world hateth you." (John 15:19)

An anti-Semite seeks to justify his hatred on the ground that the Jews are our enemies. Even if they were, is not a Christian supposed to love his enemies? "Love your enemies: do good to them that hate you: and pray for them that persecute and calumniate you: That you may be the children of your Father who is in heaven, who maketh his sun to rise upon the good, and bad, and raineth upon the just and the unjust." (Matt. 5:44-45)

Few people on the face of the earth suffered as much in recent years as the Jews. Shall Christians despise them who through suffering have become more like our Master than they themselves become through their hate and criticism?

138

Our Blessed Lord in the story of the Good Samaritan told the Jew to love his neighbor — who, in that particular instance, was a despised alien and half-breed. The Jew today is my neighbor. I may not hate him whom Christ ordered me to love.

How does the Christian ever expect the Jew to accept the Christian code unless he, the Christian, acts like a Christian? Hating the Jew will do more harm to the Christian soul than it will ever do to the Jew.

If a Christian loves the land that was sanctified by the feet of the Saviour, he ought also to love the people from whom came His Christ, the Saviour of the world.

On September 25, 1928, the decree of the Holy Office stated: "The Catholic Church habitually prays for the Jewish people who were the bearers of divine revelation up to the time of Christ: This, despite, indeed, an account of their subsequent blindness. Actuated by this love, the Apostolic See has protected this people against unjust oppression, and just as every kind of envy and jealousy among the nations must be disapproved, so in an *especial manner* must be that hatred which is generally termed anti-Semitism.

The Jews are to be no exceptions to the words of Our Lord: "All things therefore whatsoever you would that men should do to you, do you also to them. For this is the law and the prophets." (Matt. 7:12)

The disintegration of Christianity is not to be laid at the door of the Jews. Those who had most influence in robbing minds of the Divinity of Christ, by ridicule, slander, or by denying His existence, were not Jews: Voltaire, Rousseau, Hume, Kant, Hegel, Schleiennacher, Schopenhauer, Feuerbach, Friedrich Strauss, Neitzsche, Buechner, Haeckel, Drews, and the thousand lesser lights of today.

Anti-Semitism is anti-Christianity.
If a Jew has violated any of the laws of the State, the State may punish him for having done so; but the State may not do so simply because he is a Jew.

Germany did not become more Christian, more moral, and more human after its elimination of the Jews.

"I am a Jew. Hath not a Jew eyes? hath not a Jew hands, organs, dimensions, senses, affections, passions? Fed with the same food, hurt with the same weapons, subject to the same diseases, healed by the same means, warmed and cooled by the same winter and summer, as a Christian is?"

Shakespeare: Merchant of Venice

FRIENDSHIP OF JEWS
WITH CHRISTIANS

Dr. Cecil Roth, Jewish historian, addressing the Zionist Forum in Buffalo, New York, February 25, 1937, said: "We Jews who have suffered so much from prejudices, should rid our minds of prejudices and learn the facts. The truth is that the Popes and the Catholic Church from the earliest days of the Church were never responsible for physical persecution of Jews, and only Rome, among the capitals of the world, is free from having been a place of Jewish tragedy. For this, we Jews must have gratitude."

A Jew knows that anti-Semitism is not due to Christianity, because he knows that his people were persecuted before the advent of Christianity.

A Jew will never say that a child in a Catholic School or Protestant Sunday School is taught "to hate the Jews because they crucified Christ." The fact is each child is taught to beat his own breast, and to accuse himself, because *his sins* were the cause of that crucifixion.

The primary meaning of the crucifix to every Christian is: *I* sold the Lord; *I* betrayed Him; *I* crucified Him. "Now when you sin thus against the brethren, and wound their weak conscience, you sin against Christ." (1 Cor. 8:12)

No Christian hates the Jews because of the Crucifixion related in the Gospels — any more than the British hate the Americans because of the Declaration of Independence.

A Jew knows it is just as unreasonable to say the Christian is made to hate the Jew whenever the Christian speaks of Calvary, as it is to say that Americans are told to hate the English whenever Americans sing the Star-Spangled Banner.

A Jew knows that a good Christian is taught to love his neighbor and to love his enemies. Whenever therefore he falls from that ideal, and hates his fellowman, it is not because he is Christian, but because *he is not.*

A Jew knows that today all religions are persecuted. No race and no faith has a monopoly on persecution. Protestants have been persecuted in Germany, and Catholics, like the Jews, have been persecuted in every age.

No one has a right to talk on the subject of persecution unless he condemns it wherever he finds it, and irrespective of who is persecuted, whether it be a Jew, a Protestant, or a Catholic. Persecution is not essentially anti-Semitic, it is not essentially anti-Christian. It is anti-human.

Over-sensitiveness is a great barrier to friendly relations. Not every Jew is a saint and not every Christian is Christ-like. If then a Christian deplores that a particular Jew publishes filthy books disruptive of morality, the Jews must not accuse the Christian of being anti-Semitic; and because a Jew deplores the social or political injustice of a particular Christian, the Christians must not retort that the Jew is anti-Christian, or a Communist.

Christianity cannot be anti-Semitic, because it honors such Jews as Abraham, Isaac, Jacob, Moses, David. Were not the twelve Apostles Jews? Was not the first Pope a Jew? Does not the Church use the Old Testament as much as the Synagogue does? Have not its scholars defended the authenticity of the Old Testament?

"The hatred of the Jews and the hatred of the Christians springs from a common source, from the same recalcitrance of the world which desires to be wounded neither with the wounds of Israel for its movement in time, nor by the Cross of Jesus for eternal life." (Jaques Martain)

The Jew and the Christian begin to hate one another at that moment when both look for *external* causes of their misery, the Jew putting all the blame on the Christian story of the Crucifixion, and the Christian putting all the blame on the Jews.

FRIENDSHIP OF JEWS WITH CHRISTIANS

The Jew and the Christian begin to love one another when both look for the *internal* causes of their misery; that is, their sins and their forgetfulness of the moral law of God.

There is no Jew in the world who loves God and hates Christians, and there is no Christian in the world who truly loves God-made-man and hates Jews. Anti-Christianity and anti-Semitism are the yardsticks of our mutual failure to be religious.

Someday we hope to see a parade with the Jews carrying banners protesting against the persecution of Christians, and Christians carrying banners protesting against the persecution of the Jews.

The glory of the Jews is the Law they received from God. The greatest bond of unity between Jews and Christians is the keeping of the commandments of God:

I am the Lord thy God, who brought thee out of the land of Egypt, out of the house of bondage. Thou shalt not have strange gods before me.

Thou shalt not take the name of the Lord thy God in vain: for the Lord will not hold him guiltless that shall take the name of the Lord his God in vain.

Remember thou keep holy the sabbath day.

Honor thy father and thy mother, that thou mayest be longlived upon the land which the Lord thy God will give thee.

Thou shalt not kill.

Thou shalt not commit adultery. Thou shalt not steal.

Thou shalt not bear false witness against thy neighbor.

Thou shalt not covet thy neighbor's house: neither shalt thou desire his wife, nor his servant, nor his handmaid, nor his ox, nor his ass, nor anything that is his.

FRIENDSHIP OF CATHOLICS WITH PROTESTANTS

Protestantism began a little over four hundred years ago. A reformation was needed. Not the reformation of *faith* which disrupted Christian unity, but a reformation of *morals* which the Church initiated at the Council of Trent.

It would therefore be well for Catholics to recall the warning words of Cardinal Pole delivered during those trying times: "We may wish to deny that we have given birth to these heresies which are everywhere rife, because we ourselves have not uttered any heresy. Nevertheless, if we have not tilled our field as we ought — if we have not sowed — if we took no pains at once to root up the springing weeds — we are no less to be reckoned their cause than if we ourselves had sowed them.... Because the salt has lost its savor we are suffering justly, yet not for the sake of justice."

The best attitude a Catholic can take to a Protestant is to live up to the spiritual life of the Church, that non-Catholics seeing Christ reflected in their lives may desire to see that happiness fulfilled in them.

When men are starving you need not tell them to avoid poison, nor even to eat bread. One need only give nourishment and the laws of life will do the rest. In the religious sphere, in like manner, it is wrong to concentrate exclusively on pointing out errors. It is better to speak of the fulness of the life of Christ, and the grace of God will do the rest.

Be not more Catholic than the Church, for the Church does not call all Protestants formal "heretics." "If their ignorance is morally invincible they are not to be called heretics or guilty in the eyes of God," says the official teaching of the Church.

Leo XIII, in a letter to the Episcopalian Archbishops of Canterbury and York, wrote: "We indeed allow that those who are separated from Catholic unity, and have been imbued with other doctrines from their youth up, may be sincere and in good faith, so long as the truth is not suitably or sufficiently set clear to them. The one judge of the secrets of hearts is God."

The church officially calls those not of the faith "our separated brethren."

The bad Catholic who gives no glory to God, and offends Him, is heading for eternal loss. The non-Catholic who gives glory to God, according to the light of his conscience, is in his way to be saved. It ill-behooves a Catholic to act like the elder son when the prodigal came home. God is more anxious to see all His sheep in "one fold" than we are.

A Catholic must be very intolerant about the truths of His Faith, for the truths are God's and he has no rights over them. But he must be very tolerant to those who do not share that truth for God is the judge of hearts.

"Far be it from the members of the Catholic Church to exhibit any enmity in any way to strangers to the true faith and Catholic unity through no fault of their own. Rather let them fulfill all the duties of

Christian Charity toward them, above all to the poor, the sick, and those afflicted in any way amongst them." (Pius IX, 1863)

No Catholic may rejoice at the vast increase in religious indifference. It is never permitted to wish that what we believe to be impoverished should be impoverished still more. If a man were hungry, would we want him to die of hunger? Any decline in the belief of the Doctrine of Christ among our separated brethren is to some extent a loss to the Church, and to the world.

If we Catholics believed all the lies and calumnies that are told about the Church, we would hate it ten times more than bigots do. The enemies of the Church often do not hate the Church: they only hate what they erroneously believe to be the Church.

Catholics often make the great mistake of believing that they are right because of their superior understanding. No! If they enjoy the fulness of faith it is because of a gift of God.

On the other hand, Catholics may erroneously believe that others are wrong through their own fault. No! Many of them are living up to the dictates of their consciences as they see the light.

There is no religion on the face of God's earth that does not possess some truth. Instead of concentrating on error, Catholics should take hold of that segment of truth and complete the circle by revealing the fulness of the Truth and Love of Christ.

Chesterton once said that no Protestant could ever keep him out of the Catholic Church. Only a bad Catholic who gave scandal could do it.

No Catholic may ever compromise a single truth of His Church, for Truth is of God's making, not ours. But though he is as intolerant about Christ's truth as he is about two and two making four, he must be tolerant, kind, and charitable to all persons who do not share his faith, or are even opposed to it. The foundation of Catholic tolerance is not indifference to truth, but Faith, Hope, and Charity.

We have been sent into the world not to condemn, but through love to bring all men to Christ.

No bigot is to be regarded as beyond conversion. Saint Paul was a bigot. No sinner is to be regarded as too vile for union with Our Lord. Mary Magdalen was a sinner.

"By these shall all men know that you are my disciples, if you have love one for another. (John 13:35)

FRIENDSHIP OF NON-CATHOLICS WITH CATHOLICS

Judge the Catholic Church not by those who barely live by its spirit, but by the example of those who live closest to it. Art is best known through its highest representatives, not through those who daub.

The correct definition of a good Catholic is a Catholic who takes the salvation of his soul seriously.

A Catholic believes that religion is not only individual but social; that the individual receives his religion from the spiritual community or the Church, and not the other way around. It is not the union of individual believers which makes a Church; it is the Church which begets, sustains, and nourishes the individual believer.

A Catholic believes that the common life of religion is not a human fellowship, but is a fellowship of consecrated persons.

This fellowship is both vertical and horizontal; vertical because God is its Author, horizontal because it embraces all men who are "partakers of the Divine Life."

In other words, fellowship with man is impossible without fellowship with God. Men cannot be brothers unless they have God as their common father, and God is not a Father unless He has a Son, according to whose Image we are made and in whose Spirit we are quickened and united.

A Catholic believes that what the world calls "charity," or material kindness to neighbor, does not really become charity until self-giving to the brethren is based on the self-giving of God to us; for that reason, it is a direct product of His grace.

"Therefore, whether you eat or drink, or whatsoever else you do, do all for the glory of God." (1 Cor. 10:31) "For you know the grace of our Lord Jesus Christ, that being rich he became poor, for your sakes; that through his poverty you might be rich." (2 Cor. 8:9)

A Catholic believes that the Church is not an institution but a life; that it was not formed from the outside in, by Our Lord calling men together to form an organization, but from the inside out, by Our Lord sending His Spirit and thus making them one because they had one soul, the Holy Spirit.

A Catholic believes that, since his Church is Christ-made, it may not be man-unmade. He believes, too, that it never suits the particular mood of any age, because it was made for all ages.

A Catholic knows that if the Church married the mood of any age in which it lived, it would be a widow in the next age. The mark of the true Church is that it will never get on well with the passing moods of the world: "I have chosen you out of the world, therefore the world hateth you." (John 15:19)

The normal adult approach to the Catholic religion does not begin with faith, but with reason and history. What credit is to business, that faith is to a Catholic. There must be a reason for extending credit and there must be a reason for faith. Hence Saint Peter said: "But sanctify the Lord

Christ in your hearts, being ready always to satisfy every one that asketh you a reason of that hope which is in you." (1 Pet. 3:15)

A Catholic may sin as badly as anyone else, but no genuine Catholic ever denies he is a sinner. A Catholic wants his sins forgiven — not excused or sublimated.

A Catholic believes that Our Lord is present in the Eucharist in every Catholic church. That is why he tips his hat when he passes a church. That is why he genuflects when he enters the church. That is why there are kneeling benches in church; for adoration is physically expressed by the humility of kneeling.

A Catholic believes that the only true progress in the world consists in the diminution of the traces of original sin.

A Catholic believes that remarriage after divorce and artificial birth control are wrong, not simply because the Church has so decreed, but because these practices are opposed to the natural law and to the supernatural law of Christ.

Catholics build their own schools, while paying taxes for non-religious schools, because they want their children to be educated in the love of Christ and His moral law, and thus to save their souls and become worthy citizens of their country.

A Catholic does not believe that man can forgive sins, but he does believe that God can forgive sins *through man.* Christ communicated to His Church: "Whose sins you shall forgive, they are forgiven them; and whose *sins* you shall retain, they are retained." (John 20:23)

FRIENDSHIP WITH ALL PEOPLES, RACES, CLASSES AND COLORS

In every single instance hatred against any person is at bottom a *want* of religion.

Hatred of one's fellowman is an impediment to friendship with God. Love of God and of neighbor are inseparable. "If therefore thou offer thy gift at the altar, and there thou remember that thy brother hath anything against thee; Leave there thy offering before the altar, and go first to be reconciled to thy brother: and then coming thou shalt offer thy gift." (Matt. 5:23-24)

Our Blessed Lord in His preaching canceled all snobberies of race and blood and color. When His Mother and relatives came to seek Him, He looked at them and said: "Behold my mother and my brethren. For whosoever shall do the will of my Father, that is in heaven, he is my brother, and sister, and mother." (Matt. 12:49-50) From that point on the new relationship between men was to be grounded on the will of God.

We will never regard all our fellowmen as brothers until we recognize God as our Father: Humanism is dying because it has severed its affection for humanity from its roots which are in God.

The true Christian will see Our Lord's Incarnation prolonged in every human need: "I was in prison and you visited me." Touch any human being in the world — anyone whether he be a Communist, a Mohammedan, a Negro, a Buddhist, a Japanese — and you touch a person for whom Christ died, even though he knows it not.

One day the enemies of Our Lord came to Him and said, "Master, we know that thou speakest and teachest rightly: and thou dost not respect any person, but teachest the way of God in truth" (Luke 20:21). Even his enemies recognized that fundamental principle of His teaching — the sovereign worth of every person in the world. Karl Marx said an individual man had no value unless he belonged to the revolutionary class. Our Lord said a man had a value regardless of his class. "Thus, therefore, shall you pray: *Our* Father who art in heaven." (Matt. 6:9)

Standing on the Hill of Mars dedicated to the god of war, St. Paul announced to the Greeks, who felt themselves superior: "God ... made the world, and all things therein; he being Lord of heaven ... hath made of one, all mankind, to dwell upon the whole face of the earth, determining appointed times, and the limits of their habitation." (Acts 17:24-26)

Blood transfusions prove that though there are four types of blood, it makes absolutely no difference from what race or color the blood be taken, so long as it is the right type.

In the new creation of Divine Grace:

There are no racial distinctions: "There is neither Gentile nor Jew." (Col. 3:11)

No physical distinction: There is neither "circumcision nor uncircumcision." (Col. 3:11)

No cultural distinction: There is neither "Barbarian nor Scythian." (Col. 3:11)

No social distinction: There is neither "bond nor free." (Col. 3:11)

"But Christ is all and in all." (Col. 3:11)

The accidents of life, such as political position, wealth, education, are not occasions for pride, but opportunities for service: "To reveal his Son in me, that I might preach him among the Gentiles, immediately I condescended not to flesh and blood." (Gal. 1:16)

When a slave, Onesimus, came to St. Paul and was converted, Paul sent him back to his owner, Philemon, with the reminder that he was no longer a slave, but a brother through sharing Christ's grace: "Not now as a servant, but instead of a servant, a most dear brother, especially to me: but how much more to thee both in the flesh and in the Lord?" (Philemon 1:16)

Is it any wonder that Nietzsche, who hated Christ, should write: "Christianity has waged a deadly war against the distance between man and man. And if this belief of the privileges of the many makes revolutions and continues to make them, it is Christianity which is responsible. Christianity is the revolt of all that creeps on the ground against that which is elevated."

The basic reason why Communism is wrong is because it insists on the privilege of class; Nazism is wrong because it insists on the privilege of race; Fascism is wrong because it insists on the privilege of nation. Hence in theory all are anti-Christian. Think of what a revolution Christianity can be to India if the sixty million untouchables find themselves capable of becoming "children of God and heirs of heaven."

Because every person is either potentially or actually a child of God, reverence must be shown to every human being in the world:

Reverence for those whom we regard as inferior and whom we ridicule as fools because they are not of our race or class or color: "But I say to you, that whosoever is angry with his brother, shall be in danger of the judgment. And whosoever shall say to his brother, Raca, shall be in danger of the council. And whosoever shall say, Thou fool, shall be in danger of hell fire." (Matt. 5:22)

Reverence for women

"You have heard that it was said to them of old: Thou shalt not commit adultery. But I say to you, that whosoever shall look on a woman to lust after her, hath already committed adultery with her in his heart." (Matt. 5:27-28)

Reverence for the purity of our own mind and heart

"And if thy right eye scandalize thee, pluck it out and cast it from thee: for it is expedient for thee that one of thy members should perish, rather than that thy whole body be cast into hell. And if thy right hand scandalize thee, cut it off, and cast it from thee: for it is expedient for thee that one of thy members should perish, rather than that thy whole body go into hell." (Matt. 5:29-30)

Reverence for wife

In vain will men expect nations to keep international treaties, if they break domestic treaties: "What therefore God hath joined together let no man put asunder." (Matt. 19:6) "But I say to you, that whosoever shall put away his wife, excepting for the cause of fornication, maketh her to commit adultery: and he that shall marry her that is put away, committeth adultery." (Matt. 5:32)

Reverence for peace

"You have heard that it hath been said: An eye for an eye, and a tooth for a tooth. But I say to you not to resist evil: but if one strike thee on thy right cheek, turn to him also the other." (Matt. 5:38, 39)

Reverence for those who have a right to command

"Servants, be obedient to them that are your lords according to the flesh, with fear and trembling, in the simplicity of your heart, as to Christ." (Eph. 6:5)

Reverence for the needy

"Give to him that asketh of thee, and from him, that would borrow of thee turn not away." (Matt. 5:42)

Reverence for enemies

"You have heard that it hath been said, Thou shalt love thy neighbour, and hate thy enemy. But I say to you, Love your enemies: do good to them that hate you: and pray for them that persecute and calumniate you: That you may be the children of your Father who is in heaven, who maketh his sun to rise upon the good, and bad, and raineth upon the just and the unjust." (Matt. 5:43-45)

The fingers of others which we refuse to grasp in handshake will on the day of Judgment bar our way into the Kingdom of Heaven.

True Christian greatness is measured not by superiority, but by service: "And he that will be first among you, shall be your servant." (Matt. 20:27) The greatest race on earth is the race that renders the most service to others in the name of God.

To one who hated his people that great Colored leader, Booker Washington, once said: "I will allow no man to degrade my life by causing me to hate him." There is a truly Christian resolution.

"And they sung a new canticle, saying: Thou art worthy, O Lord, to take the book, and to open the seals thereof; because thou wast slain, and hast redeemed us to God, in thy blood, out of every tribe, and tongue, and people, and nation. And hast made us to our God a kingdom and priests, and we shall reign on the earth." (Rev. 5:9-10)

"Who would imagine, as we see men thus filled with a hatred of one another, that they are all of one common stock, all of the same nature, all members of the same human society? Who would recognize brothers whose Father is in heaven?" (Benedict XV)

"We confess that we feel a special paternal affection, which is certainly inspired of Heaven, for the Negro people dwelling among you; for in the field of religion and education, we know that they need special care and comfort and are very deserving of it. We, therefore, invoke an abundance of heavenly blessing and we pray fruitful success for those whose generous zeal is devoted to their welfare." (Pius XII, *Letter to the American Hierarchy.*)

NECESSARY BASIS OF LOVE OF NEIGHBOR: LOVE OF GOD

The solution of the problem of tolerance is not the carrying on of anti-hate campaigns for, unless there is love, how can hate be abolished; nor by interpreting tolerance as indifference to truth and by whittling down God's revelation to fit those who no longer believe in revelation. The discords and hates among classes and races and creeds can be sublimated and abolished only by a love of God. In order to cultivate that love of God, we invoke the appeal of those who know something about it to encourage us in the art of Divine Friendship:

"Abide in me, and I in you. As the branch cannot bear fruit of itself, unless it abide in the vine, so neither can you, unless you abide in me. I am the vine; you the branches: he that abideth in me, and I in him, the same beareth much fruit: for without me you can do nothing. ...

"As the Father hath loved me, I also have loved you. Abide in my love. If you keep my commandments, you shall abide in my love; as I also have kept my Father's commandments, and do abide in his love. ... You are my friends, if you do the things that I command you. ...

"These things I command you, that you love one another. If the world hate you, know ye, that it hath hated me before you. If you had been of the world, the world would love its own: but because you are not of the world, but I have chosen you out of the world, therefore the world hateth you.

"Remember my word that I said to you: The servant is not greater than his master. If they have persecuted me, they will also persecute you: if they have kept my word, they will keep yours also." (John 15:4-20)

"These things Jesus spoke, and lifting up his eyes to heaven, he said: Father, the hour is come, glorify thy Son, that thy Son may glorify thee ... I pray not that thou shouldst take them out of the world, but that thou shouldst keep them from evil.

They are not of the world, as I also am not of the world. Sanctify them in the truth. Thy word is truth. As thou hast sent me into the world, I also have sent them into the world. And for them do I sanctify myself, that they also may be sanctified in truth.

"And not for them only do I pray, but for them also who through their word shall believe in me, that they all may be one, as thou, Father, in me, and I in thee; that they also may be one in us, that the world may believe that thou has sent me.

"And the glory which thou hast given me, I have given to them; that they may be one, as we also are one: I in them and thou in me; that they may be made perfect in one: and the world may know that thou hast sent me, and hast loved them as thou hast also loved me. ... And I have made known thy name to them, and will make it known, that the love wherewith thou hast loved me, may be in them, and I in them." (John 17:9-26)

"Who then shall separate us from the love of Christ? Shall tribulation? or distress? or famine? or nakedness? or danger? or persecution? or the sword? (As it is written: *For thy sake,* we *are put to death all the day long. We are accounted as sheep for the slaughter.)* But in all these things we overcome because of him, that hath loved us. For I am sure that neither death, nor life, nor angels, nor principalities, nor powers, nor things present, nor things to come, nor night, nor height, nor depth, nor any other creature shall be able to separate us from the love of God, which is in Christ Jesus our Lord." (Rom. 8:35-39)

"But flesh and blood, this vessel of clay, this earthen dwelling place, when shall it attain at last to ... [love]? When shall it feel affection like this, so that inebriated with divine love, forgetful of self, and become to itself like a broken vessel, it may utterly pass over into God, and so adhere to Him as to become one spirit with Him?...

"Blessed and holy should I call that man to whom it has been granted to experience such a thing in this mortal life, were it *only* rarely, or even but once, and this, so to speak, in passing, and for the space of a moment. For, in a certain manner to lose thyself, as though thou wert not, and to be utterly unconscious of thyself, and to be emptied of thyself, and brought almost to nothing ... that pertains to the life of Heaven and not to the life of human affection.

"And if indeed any mortal is occasionally admitted to this, in passing, as I have said, and only for a moment, then straightway the wicked world begins to envy him, and the evil of the day disturbs, this body of death becomes a burden, the necessity of flesh provokes, the weakness of the corruption does not endure it, and what is even more insistent than these, fraternal charity recalls.

"Alas! he is compelled to return into himself, to fall back into his own and miserably to exclaim: 'Lord, I suffer violence, do Thou answer for me'; and this 'Unhappy man that I am, who shall deliver me from the body of this death?'

"Nevertheless, since the Scripture saith that God hath made all things for Himself (Prov. 16:4) the creature will surely at some time confirm itself and bring itself into harmony with its author.

"Some day then we shall come to love as He loves; so that even as God willed all things to exist only for Himself, so we too may will to have been and to be, neither ourselves nor naught else save equally for His sake, to serve His Will alone, and not our pleasure.

"Truly, not the appeasing of our necessity, nor the obtaining of felicity will delight us so much as that His Will shall be fulfilled in us and concerning us; which to we daily ask in our prayer when we say: Thy Will be done on earth as it is in heaven.

"O, holy and chaste love! O sweet and tender affection! O pure and perfect intention of the will ... surely so much the more perfect and pure as there is in it nothing now mixed of its own, the more sweet and tender as naught is felt but what is divine. Thus to be affected is to become Godlike." (St. Bernard, *De diligendo Deo*)

"The soul then, being thus inwardly recollected, in God or before God, now and then becomes so sweetly attentive to the goodness of the well-beloved, that her attention seems not to be attention, so purely and delicately is it exercised; as it happens to certain rivers, which glide so calmly and smoothly that beholders and such as float upon them, seem neither to see nor feel any motion, because the waters are not seen to ripple or flow at all. ...

"Even human lovers are content, sometimes, with being near or within sight of the person they love without speaking to her, and without even distinctly thinking of her or her perfections, satiated as it were, and satisfied to relish this dear presence, not by any reflection they make upon it, but by a certain gratification and repose which their spirit takes in it. ...

"Now this repose sometimes goes so deep in its tranquillity that the whole soul and all its powers fall as it were asleep, and make no movement nor action whatever, except the will alone, and even this does no more than receive the delight and satisfaction which the presence of the well-beloved affords.

"And what is yet more admirable is, that the will not even perceives the delight and contentment which she receives, enjoying it insensibly, being not mindful of herself, but of Him whose presence gives her this pleasure, as happens frequently when, surprised by a light slumber, we only hear indistinctly what our friends are saying around us, or feel their caresses almost imperceptibly, not feeling that we feel." (St. Francis De Sales, *Treatise on the Love of God*)

'What a man cannot amend in himself or others, he must bear with patience, till God ordains otherwise.

"Think, that perhaps it is better so for thy trial and patience; without which our merits are of little worth.

'Thou must, nevertheless, under such impediments, earnestly pray that God may vouchsafe to help thee, and that thou mayest bear them well.

"If any one, being once or twice admonished, does not comply, contend not with him; but commit all to God, that his will may be done, and that he may be honoured in all his servants, who knows how to convert evil into good.

"Endeavour to be patient in supporting the defects and infirmities of others, of what kind soever; because thou also hast many things which others must bear withal.

"If thou canst not make thyself such a one as thou wouldst, how canst thou expect to have another according to thy liking?

"We would willingly have others perfect, and yet we mend not our own defects.

"We would have others strictly corrected, but are not willing to be corrected ourselves.

"The large liberty of others displeases us, and yet we would not be denied anything we ask for.

"We are willing that others should be bound up by laws, and we suffer not ourselves by any means to be restrained.

"Thus it is evident how seldom we weigh our neighbor in the same balance with ourselves

"If all were perfect, what then should we have to suffer from others for God's sake?

"But now God has so disposed things, that we may learn to bear one another's burdens; for there is no man without defect: no man without his burden: no man sufficient for himself; no man wise enough for himself; but we must support one another, comfort one another, assist, instruct, and admonish one another.

"But how great each one's virtue is, best appears in occasions of adversity; for occasions do not make a man frail, but show what he is." (Thomas à Kempis, *Imitation of Christ*)

"God asks you only two things, the one is to love Him, the other is to love our neighbor. That is, therefore, what we have to strive for; in accomplishing this perfectly, we shall be doing His Will and shall be united to Him. ... That is the aim, but are we sure of attaining it?

"The most certain sign by which we may know if we are faithfully practicing these two commandments, is in my opinion, if we have a true and genuine love for our neighbor. For we cannot know for certain to what extent we love God, although there are many signs by which we may judge this; but we see much more clearly where the love of our neighbor is concerned.

"It is then extremely important to consider carefully the disposition of our soul and our outward behavior towards our neighbor. If, both interiorly and exteriorly, all is perfect, then we can be well assured, for considering the depravation of our nature, we could never love our neighbor perfectly unless we had within us a great love for God." (St. Teresa, in Marmion, *Christ the Life of the Soul*)

"I am sure that many souls will here find the reason of the difficulties, the sadness, the want of expansion in their inner life; they do not give themselves enough to Christ in the person of His members; they hold themselves back too much.

"If they would but give, it would be given to them and given abundantly; for Jesus Christ will not let Himself be outdone in love; if they would overcome their selfishness and give themselves generously to their neighbor for God's sake, Christ would give Himself to them in His fulness; if they would forget themselves, Christ would take the care of them upon Himself, and Who better than He can lead us to beatitude?

"It is not a small thing to love our neighbor always and unfailingly; it needs strong and generous love. Although the love of God is in itself, on account of the transcendence of its object, more perfect than the love of our neighbor, yet, as the motive ought to be the same in the love we bear to God and that we bear to our neighbor, often the act of love towards our neighbor requires more intensity and gains more merit.

"Why is this? Because God, being Himself Goodness and Beauty, and having shown infinite love towards us, by His grace urges us to love Him; as for our neighbor, there is always the probability of meeting in him — or in ourselves – with obstacles resulting from the differences of interest that arise between us.

"These difficulties require from the soul more fervor, more generosity, more forgetfulness of self and one's own feelings and personal desires: that is why, if love towards our neighbor is to be maintained, there is more need of effort.

"In like manner, the supernatural love that is exercised toward our neighbor, despite repugnances, antipathies, or natural dissimilarity, manifests, in the soul possessing this love, a greater intensity of Divine life.

"I do not fear to say that one who yields himself supernaturally and unreservedly to Christ in the person of his neighbor, loves Christ greatly and is infinitely loved by Him; he will make great progress in union with Our Lord. While if you meet with one who devotes much time to prayer and, in spite of that, voluntarily shuts up his compassion against the necessities of his neighbor, you may hold it for certain that there is much illusion in his life of prayer.

"For the object of prayer is to yield the soul to the Divine Will; and if the soul shuts out the neighbor, it also shuts out Christ and fails to comply with Christ's most sacred desire: *Ut unum sint, ut sint consummati in unum.* True sanctity manifests itself by charity and the entire gift of self." *(Idem)*

"I had never before fathomed the words of Our Lord: 'The second commandment is like to the first: Thou shalt love thy neighbor as thyself.' I had laboured above all to love God, and it was in loving Him that I discovered the hidden meaning of these other words: 'Not every one that saith to me: Lord, Lord! shall enter into the Kingdom of Heaven, but he that doth the will of My Father.'

"This will Our Lord revealed to me through the words of His new commandment addressed to His Apostles at the Last Supper, when He told them to love one another as He had loved them.

"I set myself to find out how He had loved His Apostles, and I saw that it was not for their natural qualities, seeing they were but ignorant men, whose minds dwelt chiefly on earthly things.

"Yet He calls them His friends, His brethren; He desires to see them near Him in the Kingdom of His Father; and to open His Kingdom to them He wills to die on the Cross, saying: 'Greater love than this no man hath, that a man lay down his life for his friends.'

"As I meditated on these divine words, I understood how imperfect was the love I bore my Sisters in religion, and that I did not love them as Our Lord does. Now I know that true charity consists in bearing all my neighbor's defects, in not being surprised at mistakes, but in being edified at the smallest virtues.

"Above all else, I have learnt that charity must not remain shut up in the heart, for 'No man lighteth a candle and putteth it in a hidden place, nor under a bushel; but upon a candlestick, that they who come in may see the light.' This candle, it seems to me, Mother, represents that charity which enlightens and gladdens, not only those who are dearest to us, but likewise all those who are of the household.

"In the Old Law when God told His people to love their neighbor as themselves, He had not yet come down upon earth; and knowing full well a man's strong love of self, He could not ask anything greater. But when Our Lord gave His Apostles a new Commandment – 'His own Commandment' – He not only required of us to love our neighbor as ourselves, but would have us love even as He does, and as He will do until the end of time." (*Idem*)

PRAYERS

PRAYER TO OBTAIN THE GRACE OF A DEVOUT LIFE

Grant me, O merciful God, to desire eagerly, to investigate prudently, to acknowledge sincerely, and to fulfill perfectly those things that are pleasing to Thee, to the praise and glory of Thy holy Name.

Do Thou, my God, order my life; and grant that I may know what Thou wilt have me to do; and give me to fulfill it as is fitting and profitable to my soul.

Grant me, O Lord my God, the grace not to falter either in prosperity or adversity; that I be not unduly lifted up by the one, nor unduly cast down by the other. Let me neither rejoice nor grieve at anything, save what either leads to Thee or leads away from Thee. Let me not desire to please anyone, nor fear to displease anyone save only Thee.

Let me never be deluded by the things that pass away, and let all things that are eternal be dear to me. Let me tire of that joy which is without Thee, neither permit me to desire anything that is for Thee; and let all repose that is without Thee be tiresome to me.

Give me, my God, the grace to direct my heart towards Thee, and to grieve continually at my failures, together with a firm purpose of amendment.

O Lord my God, make me obedient without gainsaying, poor without despondency, chaste without stain, patient without murmuring, humble without pretense, cheerful without dissipation, serious without undue heaviness, active without instability, fearful of Thee without abjectness, truthful without double-dealing, devoted to good works without presumption, ready to correct my neighbor without arrogance, and to edify him by word and example without hypocrisy.

Give me, Lord God, a watchful heart which shall be distracted from Thee by no vain thoughts; give me a generous heart which shall not be drawn downward by any unworthy affection; give me an upright heart which shall not be led astray by any perverse intention; give me a stout heart which shall not be crushed by any hardship; give me a free heart which shall not be claimed as its own by any unregulated affection.

Bestow upon me, O Lord my God, an understanding that knows Thee, diligence in seeking Thee, wisdom in finding Thee, a way of life that is pleasing to Thee, perseverance that faithfully waits for Thee, and confidence that I shall embrace Thee at the last. Grant that my life be not without penances, that I may make good use of Thy gifts in this life by Thy grace, and that I may partake of Thy joys in the glory of heaven; Who livest and reignest God, world without end. Amen. (St. Thomas Aquinas)

THE LORD'S PRAYER

Our Father who art in heaven, hallowed be thy name. Thy kingdom come. Thy will be done on earth as it is in heaven. Give us this day our daily bread. And forgive us our trespasses, as we forgive those who trespass against us. And lead us not into temptation, but deliver us from evil. Amen.

PRAYER FOR ENLIGHTENMENT

Come, Holy Ghost, fill the hearts of Thy faithful: And enkindle in them the fire of Thy love.

Send forth Thy Spirit and they shall be created: And Thou shalt renew the face of the earth.

Let us Pray:

O God, Who hast taught the hearts of the faithful by the light of the Holy Ghost, give us by the same Spirit a love and relish of what is right and just, and the constant enjoyment of His comforts. Through Christ our Lord. Amen.

PRAYER FOR GRACE TO DO THE WILL OF GOD

Grant me, most kind Jesus, Thy grace, that it may abide with me, labor with me, and persevere with me to the end.

Grant me ever to desire and to will that which is the more acceptable to Thee, and pleases Thee more dearly.

May Thy will be mine, and my will ever follow Thine, and may I be unable to will or not will anything but what Thou willest or willest not.

ACT OF CHARITY

O My God, because Thou art the highest and most perfect good, I love Thee with my whole heart, and above all things; and rather than offend Thee, I am ready to lose all things; and moreover, for Thy love I love, and will love, my neighbor as myself.

CHRIST'S PRAYER
FOR HIS DISCIPLES

I have given them thy word, and the world hath hated them, because they are not of the world; as I also am not of the world. I pray not that thou shouldst take them out of the world, but that thou shouldst keep them from evil. They are not of the world, as I also am not of the world. Sanctify them in truth. Thy word is truth. As thou hast sent me into the world, I also have sent them into the world. And for them do I sanctify myself, that they also may be sanctified in truth. And not for them only do I pray, but for them also who through their word shall believe in me; That they all may be one, as thou, Father, in me, and I in thee; that they also may be one in us; that the world may believe that thou hast sent me. And the glory which thou hast given me, I have given to them; that they may be one, as we also are one: I in them, and thou in me; that they may be made perfect in one: and the world may know that thou hast sent me, and hast loved them, as thou hast also loved me." (John 17:14-23)

PRAYER FOR OUR CIVIL AUTHORITIES

We Pray Thee, O God of might, wisdom, and justice, through whom authority is rightly administered, laws are enacted, and judgment decreed, assist, with Thy Holy Spirit of counsel and fortitude, the President of these United States, that his administration may be conducted in righteousness, and be eminently useful to Thy people over whom he presides, by encouraging due respect for virtue and religion; by a faithful execution of the laws in justice and mercy; and by restraining vice and immorality.

Let the light of Thy divine wisdom direct the deliberations of Congress, and shine forth in all the proceedings and laws framed for our rule and government; so that they may tend to the preservation of peace, the promotion of national happiness, the increase of industry, sobriety, and useful knowledge, and may perpetuate to us the blessings of equal liberty.

We recommend likewise to Thy unbounded mercy all our brethren and fellow-citizens, throughout the United States, that they may be blessed in the knowledge, and sanctified in the observance, of Thy most holy law; that they may be preserved in union, and in that peace which the world cannot give; and, after enjoying the blessings of this life, be admitted to those which are eternal. (Archbishop John Carroll)

PRAYER IN TIME OF WAR

O Lord Jesus Christ, who in Thy mercy hearest the prayers of sinners, pour forth, we beseech Thee, all grace and blessing upon our country and its citizens. We pray in particular for the President – for our Congress – for all our soldiers – for all who defend us in ships, whether on the seas or in the skies – for all who are suffering the hardships of war. We pray for all who are in peril or in danger. Bring us all after the troubles of this life into the haven of peace, and reunite us all together forever, O dear Lord, in Thy glorious heavenly kingdom.

PRAYER FOR PEACE

Give peace, O Lord, in our days; for there is none other that fighteth for us but only Thou, our God.

Let there be peace in Thy strength, O Lord.

And plenty in Thy strong places.

Let us Pray:

O God, from whom proceed holy desires, right counsels, and just works; grant unto us, Thy servants, that peace which the world cannot give, that our hearts may be devoted to Thy service, and that, being delivered from the fear of our enemies, we may pass our time in peace under Thy protection. Through Christ our Lord. Amen.

LOVE ONE ANOTHER

As the Father has loved me, so have I loved you; abide in my love.

If you keep my commandments, you will abide in my love, just as I have kept my Father's commandments and abide in his love.

These things I have spoken to you, that my joy may be in you, and that your joy may be full.

"This is my commandment, that you love one another as I have loved you.

Greater love has no man than this, that a man lay down his life for his friends.

You are my friends if you do what I command you.

No longer do I call you servants, for the servant does not know what his master is doing; but I have called you friends, for all that I have heard from my Father I have made known to you.

You did not choose me, but I chose you and appointed you that you should go and bear fruit and that your fruit should abide; so that whatever you ask the Father in my name, he may give it to you.

This I command you, to love one another.

John 15:9-17

ACKNOWLEDGMENTS

I want to thank Almighty God for the health of mind, body, and spirit to put together these reflections.

To my good wife, Isabel, my children, and my grandchildren, who keep me young at heart and are truly a blessing from God. Thank you for sharing in my joy.

I wish to express my gratitude to members of the Archbishop Fulton John Sheen Foundation in Peoria, Illinois — in particular, to the Most Rev. Daniel R. Jenky, C.S.C., Bishop of Peoria, for your leadership and fidelity to the cause of Sheen's canonization and the creation of this book.

To Julie Enzenberger, O.C.V., who repeated to me time and time again Sheen's words: "Believe the incredible, and you can do the impossible."

To my good friend and radio mentor, Terry Barber. Your passion for bringing souls to Christ through the teachings of

Archbishop Fulton J. Sheen is infectious. Your cassette tape ministry that began in the 1980's to help share the recordings and writings of Archbishop Fulton J. Sheen has enriched the lives of countless souls. Thank you for telling everyone who would listen, "Your Life is Worth Living." Full Sheen ahead my friend! Full Sheen ahead!

To the many seminarians, priests, religious, bishops, and cardinals I have met during this journey. Always remember the words of Archbishop Sheen that "The priest is not his own."

To the tens of thousands of people, I have met in my travels, giving presentations about Archbishop Fulton J. Sheen at parishes, conferences, universities, high schools, church groups, and even pubs: thank you for sharing with me your many "Sheen Stories." I truly cherish each one of them.

And lastly, to Archbishop Fulton J. Sheen, whose teachings on prayer, the sacraments, our Lord's Passion, and His Seven Last Words continue to inspire me to love God more and to appreciate the gift of the Church. His teachings and his encouragement to make a Holy Hour each day has been a true gift in my life. May I be so blessed as to imitate Archbishop Sheen's love for the saints, the sacraments, the Eucharist, and for the Mother of God. May the Good Lord grant him a very high place in Heaven!

— Al Smith

ABOUT THE AUTHOR

Fulton J. Sheen

(1895–1979)

Fulton John Sheen was born in El Paso, Illinois, in 1895. In high school, he won a three-year university scholarship, but he turned it down to pursue a vocation to the priesthood. He attended St. Viator College Seminary in Illinois and St. Paul Seminary in Minnesota. In 1919, he was ordained a priest for the Diocese of Peoria, Illinois. He earned a licentiate in sacred theology and a bachelor of canon law at the Catholic University of America and a doctorate at the Catholic University of Louvain, Belgium.

Sheen received numerous teaching offers but declined them in obedience to his bishop and became an assistant pastor in a rural parish. Having thus tested his obedience, the bishop later permitted him to teach at the Catholic University of America and at St. Edmund's College in Ware, England, where he met G. K. Chesterton, whose weekly BBC radio broadcast inspired Sheen's later NBC broadcast, The Catholic Hour (1930–1952).

In 1952, Sheen began appearing on ABC in his own series; Life Is Worth Living. Despite being given a time slot that forced him to compete with Milton Berle and Frank Sinatra, the dynamic Sheen enjoyed enormous success and in 1954 reach tens of millions of viewers, non-Catholics as well as Catholics.

When asked by Pope Pius XII how many converts he had made, Sheen responded, "Your Holiness, I have never counted them. I am always afraid if I did count them, I might think I made them, instead of the Lord."

Sheen gave annual Good Friday homilies at New York's St. Patrick's Cathedral, led numerous retreats for priests and religious, and preached at summer conferences in England.

"If you want people to stay as they are," he said, "tell them what they want to hear. If you want to improve them, tell them what they should know." This he did, not only in his preaching but also in the more than ninety books he wrote. His Peace of Soul was sixth on the New York Times bestseller list.

Sheen served as auxiliary bishop of New York (1951–1966) and as bishop of Rochester (1966–1969).

Two of his great loves were for the Blessed Mother and the Eucharist. He made a daily holy hour before the Blessed Sacrament, from which he drew strength and inspiration to preach the gospel and in the presence of which he prepared his homilies. "I beg [Christ] every day to keep me strong physically and alert mentally in order to preach His gospel and proclaim His Cross and Resurrection," he said. "I am so happy doing this that I sometimes feel that when I come to the good Lord in Heaven, I will take a few days' rest and then ask Him to allow me to come back again to this earth to do some more work."

Sheen also said that "the greatest love story of all time is contained in a tiny white host." This was the love that transformed him. His daily Eucharistic Holy Hour was legendary. From the day of his ordination to the day of his death, Sheen spent an hour a day praying in the presence of the Blessed Sacrament. From his office desk, through an open door, he could gaze upon the tabernacle at all times. His union with Christ enabled him to more fully, more accurately and more convincingly lead others to Christ in all he said and did. Sheen was a man of many talents and accomplishments, but it was Christ who enabled him to use them in the best ways.

The good Lord called Fulton Sheen home in 1979. His television broadcasts, now on tape, and his books continue his earthly work of winning souls for Christ. Sheen's cause for canonization was opened in 2002. In 2012, Pope Benedict XVI declared him "Venerable." In 2019, Pope Francis approved a miracle attributed to the intercession of the Venerable Fulton Sheen, clearing the way for his beatification.

Books Available Through Bishop Sheen Today Publishing

The Rainbow of Sorrow

The Seven Last Words

Calvary and the Mass

Love One Another

The Cross and the Beatitudes

The Cross and the Crisis

Love One Another

Victory Over Vice

The Seven Virtues

For God and Country

God and War

The Divine Verdict

God Love You

The Seven Last Words Explained

The Priest Is Not His Own

The Cross and the Crib

Philosophies at War

The Seven Last Words of Christ Explained

Father, Forgive Them for They Know Not What They Do.

This Day Thou Shall Be with Me in Paradise

Woman Behold Your Son; Behold Your Mother

My God! My God! Why Hast Thou Forsaken Me?

I Thirst

It is Finished

Father Into Your Hands I Commend My Spirit

Liberty, Equality and Fraternity

Missions and the World Crisis

Seven Words to the Cross

Seven Pillars of Peace

The Holy Hour Prayer Book

Seven Words of Jesus & Mary

www.bishopsheentoday.com

www.ingramcontent.com/pod-product-compliance
Lightning Source LLC
Chambersburg PA
CBHW021621120626
46545CB00001B/330